SOPHIE

# 100 Million Hair Ties and a Vodka Tonic

## AN ENTREPRENEUR'S STORY

Published by
**LID Publishing Limited**
The Record Hall, Studio 304,
16-16a Baldwins Gardens,
London EC1N 7RJ, UK

info@lidpublishing.com
www.lidpublishing.com

A member of:

businesspublishersroundtable.com

Printed by CPI Group (UK) Ltd, Croydon CR0 4YY
ISBN: 978-1-912555-64-2

Cover and page design: Matthew Renaudin & Caroline Li

SOPHIE TRELLES-TVEDE

# 100 Million Hair Ties and a Vodka Tonic

AN ENTREPRENEUR'S STORY

MADRID | MEXICO CITY | LONDON
NEW YORK | BUENOS AIRES
BOGOTA | SHANGHAI | NEW DELHI

*To my parents, for teaching me the importance and value of storytelling. And to the whole New Flag and invisibobble team, for the craziest and most unexpected journey. Thank you.*

*Thank you too to Lucy Handley for all of your help with the writing process.*

Note:
This is a true story. For the sake of simplicity, a few characters are composites of several people. For privacy, some people's names have been changed.

# Contents

# Preface

I'm standing in a queue at Munich airport holding a very precious piece of cargo. I've been waiting for about 20 minutes, gradually shifting forward as people scan their bags at security, and I have a sense of nervous excitement.

I'm flying to Chicago to present to a customer who I hope will want to distribute my products but, as they usually deal with much larger companies, it could be a very tough sell.

By now I'm an expert at packing a carry-on bag for all occasions; after Chicago I'm flying to Amsterdam and then China to check out our factory and discuss innovations for our next launches. But most of my luggage is taken up with tiny boxes of our product.

Finally, it's my turn and I lift my case into a large plastic tray. I wait for it to go through the X-ray machine, but it gets shunted onto the section destined for suspicious bags. I sigh and wait my turn for the security guy to inspect my bag.

"Whose is this?" asks a uniformed, middle-aged bald man.

"Mine," I say, suddenly irrationally stressed that I somehow managed to pack a gun or knife.

"What do you have in here? It shows up very strangely on the X-ray," he says as he unzips my bag. "You seem to be carrying a load of wiggly things all piled on top of each other," he says.

*Wiggly things. That's one way of putting it.*

"Um, they're hair ties?" I say as he opens my bag.

"Oh yes! I thought they looked familiar," he says, smiling in recognition. "Those spiral hair ties that don't leave a mark in your hair or give you headaches! Three in a cute plastic cube?"

I stare at him, eyebrows raised. *This old security dude with no hair knows about my hair ties?*

———

My name is Sophie Trelles-Tvede and, in 2011 when I was an 18-year-old first-year management student at the University of Warwick, I invented a spiral-shaped plastic hair tie, which I called invisibobble.

Between us, my cofounder Felix and I invested $4,000 (about £3,300) into the business, which is the equivalent of about 1,350 vodka tonics from a student bar.

Back then, we didn't even dream that our small idea for a teeny-tiny product could ever become a global brand that would eventually be sold by hairdressers, in pharmacies, high-end department stores, giant mass-market American retailers, fashion chains, European drugstores, at grocers, in beauty shops, in airports, on aeroplanes, cruise ships and even on the ice caps of Greenland (where they get transported by dog sleds). I never imagined we would change the way hair ties were made, marketed and sold, forever.

But somehow, we did. Since founding the business, we have sold more than 100 million hair ties around the world, via 85,000 retail outlets in over 70 countries. We now turn over tens of millions of dollars a year and have fundamentally changed the hair accessories category and, with it, the retail landscape for hair products.

This is the story of invisibobble.

# 1.
# Making Bikes For Goldfish

0 INVISIBOBBLES SOLD

**WHAT I LEARNED:**

- **Sometimes you have to force yourself to make friends**
- **Boredom is the mother of invention**
- **A telephone cord tied in your hair doesn't give you headaches**

Thump. Thump. Thump. Clank. Clank. Clank.

I could hear the men throwing bed frames out of the truck before I saw them. They were shouting and swearing and pulling the metal frames out, four or five at a time, and just dropping them on the ground. They looked like prison beds, and I would lie on one of them every single night as a first-year management student at the University of Warwick, UK.

My mum and I stood on the pavement as the beds were unloaded next to my accommodation building, an ugly 1970s low-rise block that was at least 20 minutes' walk from the university campus (and about my fourth choice of halls of residence). Warwick University felt about as far away from Zurich, Switzerland – where we had flown from – as you could get.

I was born in Denmark in 1993, and we moved to Switzerland when I was a baby, as my parents thought it would be a good place to start a business. I had been lucky enough to grow up in a salmon-pink house in a town by a lake, where fewer than 2,000 people lived, surrounded by green hills and cattle and the comforting smell of warm cow manure. It was the sort of place where trains run on time, cleanliness is next to godliness and the people look polished and glowing with all the alpine air.

As we walked along the long corridors of my residence hall, I felt gloomier and gloomier. International students were allowed to arrive a week early so we could get used to the peculiarities of student life, and there were very few people around. My room was at the end of a long corridor of locked doors and, as well as one of those beds, there was a sink, a wardrobe, a chair and a long wooden desk nailed to the wall. I wondered what lay ahead.

After my mum said a tearful goodbye, I realized that to ever make contact with another human, I would have to make my way to the main campus to eat the free food the university was providing. But there was one problem. I have a syndrome commonly known as 'resting bitch face,' something I inherited from my parents, so people didn't tend to warm naturally to me. I'm also quite shy and not very good at small talk (one thing I've had to get much better at), so I was dreading the effort I'd need to put in to make new friends.

I looked at my reflection in the mirror, reminded myself to smile and took a deep breath. I opened the door and immediately saw another girl in the corridor. She was French and her name was Marie, and we walked into campus together. Thank God for Marie.

I spent most of my first term partying, sleeping, concentrating on not dying from my vodka tonic-induced hangovers and learning how to deal with the filth of being a student.

About 18 of us shared a kitchen, and one day someone cooked a chicken in a massive pot on the stove and left it there. No one laid claim to the boiled bird so, after about three weeks, a few of us carried it into the corner of the room. Then we noticed some white fluff coming out of the top of it, which gradually started to grow up the wall. As a result, I spent as little time cooking as possible.

The bathrooms were even worse than the kitchen, especially on Wednesday mornings. Tuesday night was the big one at the campus club, and after several hours of shots, snogs and maybe a 2am curry, our digestive systems were up shit creek, wreaking havoc on the toilets.

I bought a bike to transport myself around, but having wheels meant I'd wait until the very last second to leave my room before pedalling my heart out to reach lectures on time. I would often arrive late, out of breath and sweating profusely. But after a few weeks I practically stopped going to lectures.

By December, I started to have horrible feelings of guilt. There was a kind of red alarm light going off in my head that had built up as a result of doing very little for an entire ten weeks. As the Christmas holidays approached, I felt ashamed and unfulfilled.

This management course at Warwick had been my dream, but the reality?

I was bored as hell.

I thought about what I could do with my time productively. Join the basketball squad? *Nah, I have a bad shoulder and a dodgy knee.* I know! Volunteer for a charity. *But would I stick to that?* How about skiing? I signed up to the university team but quit immediately when I found out they skied on AstroTurf.

I really, really need to have an interest in an activity to excel at it – otherwise, you can forget it. Desperate to find something to occupy my mind, I locked myself in my bedroom for a week in December. I sat at my desk attached to the wall, thinking about things that I could make and sell; a side project that would hopefully stop me from getting bored and feeling guilty.

One afternoon, I started thinking about how regular elastic hair bands would give me a headache. They somehow created tension on my head because the hairs pulled on my scalp, and that made it ache all over, which was really unpleasant. I wondered whether there could be some kind of creative way around that.

There was a campus party to go to that night, and the theme was 'bad taste.' You had to dress up in as ugly a costume as possible, drink a lot, and hope that your outfit would be a talking point (and also have a positive impact on my resting bitch face). On my way out, I spotted the coiled phone cord that was attached to the landline phone in my room, so I unplugged it and quickly tied it up in my hair, wrapping it around my ponytail a few times so the spiral ends stuck out. It looked perfectly ugly.

The next morning, I woke up with the phone cord still in my hair. And aside from feeling a bit fuzzy from a few vodka tonics, there was no tension from the cord tying up my ponytail.

I had no headache.

Sitting in my small, simple bedroom at Warwick University, 743 miles away from my hometown in Switzerland and more than 100 miles away from Felix, who was then my boyfriend, I wondered if – just if – I had stumbled across something interesting. I felt a small tingle in my stomach.

I, Sophie Trelles-Tvede, a student at a top management school that I worked my ass off to get into, was feeling excited about something that had nothing to do with how I expected I would feel at the end of my first term.

I was feeling a tingle of enthusiasm about a piece of coiled grey telephone cord.

I called Felix, who was studying at the University of Bath's business school, about three hours by train from Warwick.

"Iwenttoabadtastepartyandputmyhairupinatelephonecordandiwokeupjustnowwithoutaheadache!"

"What?"

"I put my hair up in a spiral telephone cord and I don't have a headache! I thought I could make hair ties out of the cord and it could be a nice side project."

There was silence. My idea must have sounded like nonsense to Felix, as if I was trying to sell earrings to dogs or make bikes for goldfish.

Eventually, he said, "How much did you spend?"

This was typical Felix. He wants details and numbers first and only gets excited once there is proof that something is going to work. I could forgive him for wondering why this seemed like a good idea.

Felix also felt frustrated with his degree. His older brother, Dani, and his business partner, Niki, were living in Munich, where Felix was from, and they were having the time of their lives as German distributors for the Tangle Teezer hairbrush. (Distributors do what it says on the tin – they buy products in bulk from a manufacturer and distribute them to various places those products can be sold, such as hair salons.)

The Tangle Teezer was well-known in the UK but not in Germany, so Dani and Niki helped the brand expand. (Before that, they were selling a blanket with arms, but it turns out there's a limited number of people who want those.) We'd heard about everything Dani and Niki were doing, learning about business and real life, and making money, too. Frankly, we were pretty envious of their success.

Felix also knew about the headaches I got from regular elastic hair bands, and once he realized that the phone cord hair tie might be able to solve that problem, he got more into the idea.

"OK," Felix said down the line. "Tell me more."

# 2.
# The Girl's Telephone Line Rubber Band

0 INVISIBOBBLES SOLD

**WHAT I LEARNED:**

- If you create a new word to name your product, you'll show up first on Google (to start with, at least)
- As students, we had nothing to lose by starting a business
- People get glory for attracting investment — but it doesn't have to be that way

Back in 2012, hair bobbles or hair ties were just pieces of fabric-covered elastic sold in packs of 30 for about £1, necessary things that women used to stick their hair up in a ponytail or tied their kid's plaits with. They were cheap and unbranded and definitely weren't hair-friendly.

As well as giving me headaches, the ends of the elastic were welded together with a tiny piece of metal, which would catch in my hair. Sometimes, I'd end up with a small clump of hair sticking up on my head and I'd grab my ponytail and pull at it to try to smooth it out. But that usually ended up just creating more bumps. Using a piece of phone cord, I didn't feel like there were any hairs hanging on for dear life as somehow they were all held smoothly together.

Experimenting with the phone cord, I then realized something else: there was no dent when I pulled it out of my hair. I have long, fine, blonde hair and regular hair ties would leave a strange-looking kink – and I knew that other people had this problem too, with various different hair types.

Over the Christmas holidays and into the new year of 2012, Felix and I became telephone-cord experts. We noticed that they came in slightly different thicknesses and sometimes the cord itself was completely circular, but mostly there was a flat side on the inside. Instinctively, I felt like the circular kind would look better and also be kinder to hair.

What we needed was someone who could make us the cord alone, without the electrical telephone cable going through it: a manufacturer who could also glue the ends of the cord together to make a circular hair tie. From the start, we wanted our product to be fundamentally different to regular hair ties. The material had to be plastic with a smooth surface that had springiness. It had to stay in shape, and it had to feel good in your hair.

But you can't Google 'telephone cord without the wire' and get a load of quality results, and it's not like doing a new version of a paperclip. There are other spiral-shaped products – spiral notebooks, the Slinky, shower hoses – but they all have metal components, which we didn't want.

We did research on Alibaba, which is a bit like a giant Chinese version of Amazon where you can buy anything from live lobsters to remote-controlled vibrators. There we found about 15 possible suppliers and emailed them with the subject line,

"Girl's telephone line rubber band," which at the time felt like the best way of explaining what we thought we wanted: a spiral-shaped rubber band hair tie, rather like a telephone cord.

Eventually we found a guy called Liang who made telephone cords as well as the wires that bodyguards wear, and we persuaded him to make our first samples. We had to negotiate a bit, as manufacturers often seemed to have minimum order quantities. So I wrote him an email, plucking numbers from thin air.

ORIGINAL MESSAGE

From: "Sophie Tvede"
To: "趙 李"
Sent: Mon, 6 Feb 2012, 7.46 AM UTC+0800
Subject: Re: Re: Girl's telephone line rubber band

**Hello Liang,**

**If you tell me how many days the delivery of the sample will take and how many days until you dispatch it, I will wire you the money within the next 24 hours via PayPal.**

**If I am satisfied with the products, we will make a test order of 15,000. If I am still satisfied, we will make an order of 200,000.**

**Thank you,**

**Sophie Trelles-Tvede**

A couple weeks later, our girl's telephone line rubber band samples arrived at my residence in Warwick. Sure enough, they were round hair ties, made of phone cord-type material that had been soldered together. They were in different thicknesses and sizes and some were made from cord that had one flat side, and some were round.

But they looked horrible.

I had imagined a tiny, colourful, spiral-shaped hair tie that felt smooth and looked cute. But instead the colours were a sickly yellow and a grim green. They stretched a lot and felt rough to touch, and they had a chemical smell. But they were all we had, so I at least had to try them.

Standing in front of the mirror, I tied one up in my hair and wobbled my head quickly from side to side.

The hair tie was still holding.

I tilted my head and shook it violently several times like I was trying to get water out of my ear.

The cord was still in place.

I moved my head round and round like a shot put athlete at the Olympics.

All good.

Then I made headbanging movements. I flicked myself in the eye with my ponytail, but the hair tie felt comfortable and stayed in place. It was maybe a bit heavy in my hair, but I felt if we could fine-tune it, it could become a really good product. I left it in my hair for an hour and there was no kink when I took it out. Crucially, I didn't get a headache.

I called Felix. (Being a guy with short hair, he had to trust me.)

"These phone cord hair ties work, you know," I said.
"Awesome. We can do this. We go big or go home."

Right from the start, Felix was very vocal about NOT having a small 'ha ha' local business. It means a small business which is for fun, rather than something that is actually supposed to support your living. We were doing this, and we were in it together.

I think that 99% of ideas stay as just that: ideas. I'd previously thought that to start your own business, you had to do the following:

- Get a bachelor's degree. Find yourself. Discover what you're interested in (three years)
- Get a master's degree. Dig into career ideas in more detail (one year)
- Get an epic job. Earn money. Have financial stability (25 years)
- Start the business you dreamed of long, long ago while at school (which at this point someone else has probably already created, so there's not much left for you to do)

Those were my preconceptions, and I think a lot of people feel that's the path to becoming an entrepreneur. But I've learned that it really doesn't have to be that way.

We were 18 when I came up with the idea for our hair ties, and I turned 19 in January 2012, which is when we started the business. But I believe if I'd waited until after a 25-year career, then the hair accessory business would never have got started. Economic and personal risk just increases as you get older and if we'd waited, I think either someone else would have invented the spiral hair tie or I would have thought the idea was too ridiculous to risk my entire professional career.

Our girl's telephone line rubber band product was kind of ridiculous, but I had faith in it. Before we could attempt to start selling it properly, we needed a name. I really wanted a brand-new word, one that felt feminine, cute, fun and went some way to explain what the product did.

It also had to be a name that, when typed into Google, produced no search results to start with. So, when the brand name was invented and people started hearing about it, the name would show up on the first page.

Felix took my brief for the name very literally.

One night, I sat in my room, cross-legged on my bed, messaging him on my BlackBerry (a now defunct type of smartphone). It went something like this:

FELIX **I've got the perfect name!**

**!** ME

**No Trace.**

**That's what you think we should call it???!
That's TWO words, not one.**

**Yes! It leaves no trace,
so, NoTrace, get it?**

**No. I want to invent a new word,
not put two existing words together!**

**TraceFree?**

**That's exactly the same concept!
Trace and Free are already words.**

**ElastiTrace!**

I wrote our ideas down. It was an uninspiring list:

No-TrAce          TraceFREE          ElastitrACE
        HairKindly          SpiralhAIR

Then I remembered that my British friend Hope always referred to hair ties as hair bobbles, a name I always thought sounded funny. And then I thought: this product leaves no trace. At some point on a February night, the word 'invisible' came into my head, and if you cut off the 'le' at the end, you could run it into the word 'bobble,' to get 'invisibobble.' So, it's like a hair tie that doesn't leave a dent.

Still sitting on my bed, I typed 'invisibobble' into Google.

*"Did you mean invisible bubble?"* Google wrote back. I clicked on the first result for 'invisible bubble' and ended up on a web page that stated: "Everyone has an invisible bubble around their bodies. The bubble limits just how close someone may approach before one feels uneasy and it also limits one's approach to another."

Much as this invisible bubble sounded like a superpower I wished I had, it was about as far away from a coiled hair tie as you could get.

There were no results for 'invisibobble.' NO results!

Maybe this word 'invisibobble' is going to follow me around for a while, I thought. Probably not, but it might, so remember this moment, I told myself.

Felix thought 'invisibobble' was acceptable, but only secondary to all the amazing suggestions he had made. But we pressed on with designing a logo. To make 'invisibobble' easier to read, we wrote 'invisi' and 'bobble' in different shades of green and made a design using the cheap, student version of Photoshop. We added "The traceless hair ring," underneath, which still appears on our packaging today.

You can have products ranging from being as complicated as nuclear reactors to as simple as stone axes, and the invisibobble spiral hair tie is definitely closer to the stone axe side of things. That doesn't make it any less of a good invention, but it sure seemed that way for a lot of friends who took the piss out of me to start with.

People really weren't sure about it when I asked for their opinion.

"It looks like a weird kind of spring."
"Won't it tangle up in your hair?"
"Did someone puke that on to you?!"

People would call it ugly because they didn't like the colours, or they'd say it didn't feel very fashionable. It was such a weird concept to put something that looked like a telephone cord in your hair when no one had ever done anything like that before.

There were some guys at university who got a £25,000 (about $30,000) grant to make an internet-connected light bulb attachment that could be dimmed remotely via a smartphone. A great idea, and they got a lot of glory for winning that grant. But there was no investment for my product, and people's reactions were sceptical at best.

Hair ties were a very low involvement and functional product, a bit like toilet paper. With toilet paper, as long as your butt is halfway clean, people are happy, give or take. It's something you need, but never look forward to buying.

But we had the opportunity to make hair ties go from the hair accessory equivalent of toilet paper into something magical that people loved and wanted – and would pay more for.

# 3.
# Mr Bernhard Stumbles Across Our Website

900 INVISIBOBBLES SOLD

**WHAT I LEARNED:**

- **Too much choice can stop people from buying stuff**
- **A blend of creativity and efficiency is essential for a start-up**
- **Knowing nothing about an industry can be an advantage to working in it**

Although I was really excited, despite all the haters, it was Felix who created deadlines for us. I'd visit him in Bath and want to hang out after we'd worked hard on invisibobble for the day, but he'd stay up late to finish the logo or write copy for our website.

The winter before we started university we'd both worked as ski instructors. In Switzerland, where I worked, they paid really well and in Austria, where Felix worked, they paid really poorly.

I was earning 25 Swiss francs (around £21 or $26) an hour excluding tips, and I didn't have to pay taxes because I made less than the minimum threshold for the year.

We saved about £1,650 each (around $2,000). Felix had needed to work much harder than me, but we never thought we'd be spending a large chunk of our life savings on thousands of tiny, brightly coloured, coiled pieces of plastic that would eventually be shipped over from China in a container.

But that's exactly what we did, because once we got to a point where we were happy with our samples, our first order of 15,000 invisibobbles with the guy from Alibaba cost us around £3,000 (or $3,800). It was a pretty big decision to invest, especially since people had largely ridiculed us, but we were sure it was the right thing to do. New shoes or a holiday could wait: this was a real idea.

This price included packaging because we needed to find a more interesting way of packing our hair ties than simply stapling them to a piece of cardboard. I'd seen packs of two nail varnishes sold in little Ziploc-type bags that I thought looked cute, so we posted one to Liang and asked him to produce 5,000 of them. We also asked him to make larger bags that would fit five and ten hair ties, and got him to print on the packages the web address we were going to buy: invisibobble.com.

We also needed everything to arrive speedily because, as much as Felix would create deadlines to make sure we kept going, we also had a real one looming: the Hair & Beauty show in Frankfurt, a large trade fair in Germany attended by buyers and hair salons, exhibiting everything from hair extensions to salon furniture. Dani and Niki's distribution business, New Flag, would have a Tangle Teezer stand there and it would be a massive opportunity to get invisibobble out to the professional hair industry. The fair was two months away.

On Saturday 17 March 2012 at 1.49am Felix emailed me, "We REALLY need these hair ties before my bro and Niki go to the hair convention. It would really get us off to a good start," he wrote. Five days later, another email came through.

From: "Felix Haffa" <felix@invisibobble.com>
To: Me
Sent: Thu, 22 Mar 2012, 1.23 AM
Subject: hihihi check out what email im sending from

Ah, Felix. He had been my boyfriend since the age of about 15, when we'd met in high school in Zurich. Before we dated, I thought he was this good-looking guy with a few close friends who would always hang out together. I don't think I ever saw him smile and found the whole group pretty intimidating and a bit arrogant.

But when we went on a school trip to Lake Garda in Italy, we started talking and, once I got to know him, I realized it was more like introversion than arrogance. When we got back to Zurich, he asked me out.

Felix says he thought I was shy and pretty, and he was scared to talk to me. And while he was very competitive about everything, sacrificing time with friends to study, I was a bit more sociable at school. But we were similar in that we were best left alone to get on with our studies. He's also the most driven person you'll ever meet, obsessed with details and always pushing to be better. These days, if we sell $1 million of something, he'll say, "Why not $2 million?" and if we get news that a deal isn't going as planned, he'll ask me about it three times a day until it gets sorted.

Felix has always been the one who wanted to get stuff done and I'm much more creative. I have a super strong focus on nurturing our brand and thinking long term, whereas Felix is much more about numbers and how we can cash in right *now*. I think you need both types for a successful business partnership, though it's made for some arguments along the way.

But there we were, in March 2012, not really knowing anything about anything because we were still teenagers, waiting for our 15,000 tiny spiral pieces of plastic and 5,000 tiny bags to travel 5,000 miles from a guy called Liang who lived somewhere in China, to Felix's parents' home in Munich, where we were heading for the Easter holidays.

Back then, our tiny hair bands were just over an inch in diameter and came in 27 different colours. We gave them names like Submarine Yellow, which was very bright, then there was a kind of sludgy colour we named Turtle Green and also a shiny blue one we called Space Blue. We were very imaginative.

Looking back, 27 colours and three pack sizes was waaaay too much to start with. It's proven that in supermarkets, the smaller the assortment of any type of product, the higher chance you have of someone buying it. So, if you have three types of jam – strawberry, raspberry and apricot – it's pretty clear what your choice is. But if you have 20 kinds of strawberry jam, 20 kinds of raspberry, 20 kinds of apricot and various mixtures of all three, it just gets so overwhelming that often people give up and don't buy anything at all.

Anyway, once everything arrived, we spread it all out on Felix's parents' living room floor, separating all 15,000 hair ties into piles of different colours like a giant, multicoloured rainbow across the carpet. We had to gradually push tables, chairs and sofas toward the walls to make more room.

We sat on the floor, crawling between the piles, packing them into invisibobble-branded bags of two, five and ten, in multiple colour combinations, as well as five and ten packs of black only. The whole house smelled like a plastic factory, and after about three days Felix's dad, who had been avoiding us, came in.

"Put. It. ALL AWAY!" he shouted, a little red in the face. I don't think Felix's parents quite realized the disruption we would cause, and they definitely didn't understand why we had such faith that anyone would actually buy a coiled hair band. We were lucky that Felix's brother rented a warehouse in Munich for New Flag, so after we'd finished packing our 15,000 hair ties, Dani let us move our stock there.

We had a name and we had our products; now, we needed a website. We used software from Shopify and took pictures of one of our friends wearing different coloured invisibobbles in her hair. Our logo matched the Turtle Green-coloured invisibobble and our homepage had a slideshow of several images: invisibobbles in our friend's ponytail, a multicoloured packet of ten, a pile of red, black and yellow hair ties, and finally, an image showing nine Turtle Green hair ties that looked like a pile of little green curled-up caterpillars.

We had information about the product, the colours, an 'about us' section, shipping options to Germany, Austria and Switzerland, and an FAQ. It actually looked pretty professional.

The day our website went live, we got our first order.

A German man called Uwe Bernhard had ordered a five-pack of mixed coloured invisibobbles for €8.49 and paid the standard shipping fee of €1.99, making a grand total of €10.48 (about £9.40 or $11.50).

Somehow, Mr Bernhard had stumbled across our website, browsed through it and decided to place an order. The feeling was amazing. Half holy shit, this is completely unique, not ever been done before, put it in a blender, shit on it, vomit on it, it's an out-of-this-world kind of a feeling (to borrow a little of Lady Gaga describing how she feels about movie director

Ryan Murphy), and the other half laughing our asses off that a man of indefinite age, hairstyle and profession had seen our invisibobbles, liked them, taken out his credit card and bought a pack.

Not that we didn't believe in invisibobble, but at the end of the day we were two bored teenagers who had no idea about what we were doing, and suddenly we had made €10 from a random dude. We were over the moon, and we put his tiny pack of invisibobbles carefully into a little cardboard box, with a hand-written delivery note and a thank you card. We hoped that if Mr Bernhard bought invisibobbles, others would too.

Somehow, the orders started coming in from there and, on a good day, we'd sell between £45 and £63 (around $55 to $70) worth of products. But we also knew that it wasn't cost effective to keep posting out small orders from a website, and to get bigger we would need to find a distributor. Dani and Niki suggested we send free packs to hair salons with their Tangle Teezer orders and hopefully the hairdressers would like them and start ordering invisibobbles too.

What we didn't know at the time was that salons often have exclusivity deals with big manufacturers like L'Oréal or Schwarzkopf where they are only allowed to sell shampoos and so on from those companies, which make brands like Kerastase and Redken. But because there was no exclusivity deal for hair accessories, getting into hair salons wasn't a problem.

If we had known these kinds of 'rules' or anything about the beauty or hair industry at all, it might have held us back, or we might have thought that putting packets of invisibobbles in with Tangle Teezers was the wrong thing to do. But being kids at the time, we knew nothing. Really, I mean we knew so little that we didn't even know that we knew nothing.

Hairdressers did like the invisibobbles we sent with the Tangle Teezers and because the hair ties are so tiny, they often found a place to fit them in. We did a deal where they could buy 100 hair ties for £46 (about $56) and we'd send them a glass fishbowl-type jar for free to put them in, so it was easy for a customer to buy a pack of hair ties after they'd had their hair done. Spending £4.60 (about $5.60) on a pack of three invisibobbles was nothing compared to what they'd probably paid for their haircut or fancy blow-dry.

And despite testing Felix's dad's patience, we managed to get packs of hair ties ready for the Frankfurt Hair Fair. I couldn't go because exam time was approaching at Warwick, but what happened blew our minds. My dad had run his own businesses and taken an interest in invisibobble, so I sent him an update.

From: Me
To: Tvede
Sent: Thu, 17 May 2012, 12.56 PM
Subject: small update

**At the fair in Frankfurt, there was a guy who owns ten hairdressers and has connections to over 600 hairdressers in Germany who showed strong interest in our hairbands.**

**He is not up for giving us a good deal, but if we get this to work, it would be amazing because we would potentially be selling our hair bands in 600 different hairdressers across the country, which is a great start. If this happens, we would get amazing publicity and get a higher chance of selling in big department stores! All super exciting.**

**Sophie**

The hairdresser guy was called Rick Vahr, and he ordered a few hundred invisibobbles to put into his own salons. If they sold well, it would be easy for him to give samples to his sales force to pass on to other salons, because our products are tiny. If that was a success, he might sign a deal with us to distribute to all 600 salons. We had 15,000 invisibobbles to shift, so we had to keep going.

# 4.

# My Dad Bet
# The House

23,000 INVISIBOBBLES SOLD

**WHAT I LEARNED:**

- **Other people's opinions can be annoying**
- **But they can also give you ideas you never dreamt of
  (thank you Debbie the hairdresser)**
- **There is no magic hair tie fairy**

For the first nine months, all I could think about was whether
our hair ties really worked and perfecting them until they were
the best they could be. I didn't want to have a situation where
people bought invisibobbles because they looked funky or weird
(in a good way) and then used them but weren't really happy.
Our invisibobbles had to be perfect.

I have long, fine, typical Nordic-type hair, and I needed to
understand how our product worked in other hair types. At the
time, we had a focus group of one – me – so I would give hair ties
to students around campus and watch while they put their hair up.

Here's how these conversations would usually go:

Me:      Hi, have you seen this new kind of hair bobble?
Student: That's a hair bobble? Won't it tangle?
Me:      Would you like to try it for free?
Student: Free? Sure! Uh, I'll probably lose it though.
Me:      Would you mind if I watched while you put your hair up now?
Student: Okaaayyyy.

When you've invented something that has never, ever been seen before, you get completely obsessed with how people use it and who wears it. And I mean obsessed. The first time we saw a woman wearing an invisibobble in a Munich park, Felix and I chased her around for ages, wide-eyed and with eyebrows raised, making high-five gestures silently behind her back. Other people could see us doing this little victory dance, but she couldn't. You can't imagine what it's like to know that someone has seen your product and spent money on it.

In all seriousness, the reason I wanted to see people use the product was to check if they felt the same way I did about it, that they found them easy to wear and that they came out of their hair easily. A couple weeks later, I'd see the same students on campus and notice that they still had their invisibobbles with them, because they would be wearing it like a bracelet, which was exactly what I was doing. That was never in our plan, but everyone just did it.

People wearing invisibobbles on their wrists showed that they were happy to use them the same way they used regular hair ties, even though they had a very different look. This gave me confidence that there was something about this product that worked, because a lot of people I told about invisibobble still weren't getting it. Girls had their way of putting their hair up, which they claimed to be happy with, and they still thought about hair ties in the same way they thought about toilet paper: a dull necessity.

To start with, our hair ties weren't amazing. They would stretch out and not spring back into shape, so we had to do a lot of refinement. But I still knew that I had solved the problem of hair dents and headaches, and I kept telling myself that if I saw the value in the product, other people would too.

I also knew that we'd need to get expert feedback on the hair ties. And this is where the hairdressers came in. We realized that not only did the product not leave dents or give people headaches, it also didn't damage people's hair when they pulled it out. This made hairdressers love it and talk to their clients about it too, and it meant we could put 'hair loving' on our packaging.

Most hairdressers would put in orders once or twice a month, but we started getting orders from one woman, Debbie, about twice a week. Maybe she had a massive salon, right in the middle of a city that was open all day and all night, or maybe she somehow had brilliant salespeople.

I sent Felix a text message on 3 September 2012.

**Debbie's done it again!** ME

FELIX **How many has she ordered this time?**

**Like, 300 packs.**

**Is she eating them like sweets?**

Turns out, she was a regular hairdresser in a regular German town using invisibobbles in a way that we'd never considered: up-dos. If someone had just had a haircut, she'd offer to give them a free up-do using our plastic hair ties. Debbie would be able to do a hairstyle using just one invisibobble instead of, say, three regular hair ties and 15 metal bobby pins.

Interesting. You see, I had one very clear goal for the benefit of the product, which was no headaches. Felix had one very clear goal, which was to make something that had the potential to be sold at scale, and he was also obsessed with producing it efficiently. And then the hairdressers were giving us all of these other angles, like the fact that the smooth surface meant it was kind to your hair, and you could be creative with up-dos. They were developing our business for us!

This became super important, because we then started working with Debbie on different hairstyles that we would film and put on YouTube; having the right kind of content is really important for new products. Felix is not a hair guy, trust me, he really isn't. But he's a business guy, and he totally got the point of working with Debbie. We still work with hairdressers now and their YouTube tutorials regularly get tens of thousands of views. Turns out that there are many more Debbies out there.

One day, about a month after the Frankfurt Hair Fair, Felix and I were back in his parents' house packing invisibobbles (in the basement this time), and Felix checked his email. There was a new message from Rick, the guy with 600 hair salons. His trial had gone well, and he wanted to place an order. We could hardly believe it: a serious businessperson saw the potential in our products, less than six months after we'd started invisibobble. We got to work, a bit like in *Snow White and the Seven Dwarfs* when the dwarfs are happily packing the diamonds they've mined, singing "Heigh-Ho" and marching in time to the music.

We ordered some more jars from Amazon, had some invisibobble stickers printed, and spent an afternoon sticking them onto the jars and filling them with a mixture of colours, as well as packing the little bags with five or ten of our hair ties. Then we carefully wrapped the jars in paper and put them in cardboard boxes ready to take to the post office the next day. There were about ten boxes and after we'd dispatched them, we texted Rick to let them know they were on the way.

Three days later, Rick texted back. About half of our lovingly wrapped jars had arrived smashed to pieces, so we went back down to the basement and started again. This time with bubble wrap and thicker cardboard boxes. We soon realized there are several types of cardboard (who knew?), and we needed a style called 'double walled,' where there are two layers of corrugated paper reinforcing each wall of the box. Not getting the packaging right had cost us time and money, but our mistake made us hyper-aware that details are important. The devil is in them.

Rick kept on placing orders, and whenever they would come through, I would write an invoice, which was one of the things I'd do during the university lectures I bothered to go to.

Perhaps the lecturers thought I was taking notes. Other management students would grin if they saw me, teasingly saying: "Oh, Sophie, you've graced us with your presence!"

While none of the tutors really knew if I skipped lectures, seminars were harder to avoid. Early on, I asked a friend to fake my signature on seminar attendance sheets, which worked to an extent. Problem was, the tutors hadn't memorized all of our names, so they'd rely on the attendance list to pick on us for questions. If you missed more than three seminars, the university would write to your parents. So, I had to go to at least some of them, but I bent the rules as much as I could.

The summer holidays came around and I went away to Barcelona with Hope and a few other girls, and this is when

Hope started to realize that invisibobble was a thing. I'd met Hope at school in Zurich and we'd become best friends – and from the start we were always very honest with each other. Every day, we'd wake up hungover and while my friends were getting ready to go to the beach, I'd be 'really annoying,' in Hope's words.

"I need to do a few tasks," I'd say.

"What tasks could you possibly need to do RIGHT NOW?" Hope would ask.

"I need to write some invoices."

Hope laughed that I was writing them out in Word, saving them as PDFs and emailing them to whoever had ordered invisibobbles. I'd be super excited and wake up at 6am to see if we'd had any orders, and then I'd type out the invoices.

By now, our order value had gone up to between about £100 and £450 (about $120 to $550) a day and, if we were lucky, one would come in for around £1,000 ($1,200). To a 19-year-old, trying to start a company in her first year of university, these sums were huge, as they would be to anyone in a tiny business like ours. But we were profitable from the start: within a couple months of starting the business, we had sold enough to make our initial £3,300 ($4,000) investment back and put any money we made into getting more invisibobbles made and fulfilling more orders.

But to my dad, these sums of money were pitiful.

You see, my dad didn't exactly have a conventional job, but instead was self-employed and always sort of did whatever he wanted to do to be successful. He was very good at trading commodities like copper, and I remember one day when I was a kid, he got off the phone and told me he'd just bought all this copper. About two weeks later, I asked why it hadn't arrived at our house.

Me:     "When does the copper get delivered, Dad?"
Dad:    "The copper doesn't get delivered."
Me:     "Why did you buy it then?"
Dad:    "No, I've just bought it temporarily, and then I'm selling it, hopefully in about two months."
Me:     "How does that work?"
Dad:    "Well, while I own the copper, the price will go up and then I can sell it for a profit."

Another time, I was sitting in the kitchen in my pajamas watching *SpongeBob* on TV, eating a sandwich, and my dad came in and sat next to me, kind of pale.

Me:     "Are you OK?"
Dad:    "I just bet the house."
Me:     "On what?"
Dad:    "Well, the Turkish lira has fallen like a rock, and now I can get really high interest and great returns if I buy it."

I won't go into the details of foreign exchange trading, but let's just say my dad sometimes made massive bets on currencies, which he didn't always win. That time he did, though, so I turned back to *SpongeBob*.

My dad's bets were usually pretty big, and me making a few hundred euros on some plastic hair ties didn't exactly impress him. He also didn't really understand that people would buy a packet of invisibobbles and then buy them again. It wasn't until he waited in queues in airports and saw more and more women with them in their hair or on their wrists that it started to dawn on him that they were popular, and that people wanted them in different colours (and different sizes, when we went on to make them). My dad was not made for the world of women's accessories.

He also didn't really think about how the chicken he was eating for dinner got to the supermarket or where his toothpaste was made. I think for him, all of those were things that just existed. It's as if the couch in our living room just appeared there by magic, as if God had said, "Here's your couch now!"

Physical goods require an enormous amount of handling and many people who work with virtual goods such as software or finance understandably don't realize the extent of that. And I still have people ask me whether I do my job full-time, as if invisibobbles appear in stores by magic, delivered by the hair tie fairy.

# 5.
# Suddenly,
# We Were 22

55,000 INVISIBOBBLES SOLD

**WHAT I LEARNED:**

- **People might not take you seriously if you have a business but look like children**
- **Weird-looking products can catch on**
- **Thinking about packaging in a completely different way can be absolutely critical for success**

In September 2012, when Felix and I started our second year of university, it became clear that we needed to get a bit more organized. We had already sold around £46,000 (about $56,500) worth of invisibobbles, mainly to hairdressers in the UK and Germany, and we gave ourselves until the end of the year to either make the business work or give up and start something else.

I was still alive after my first year in halls of residence, surviving the prison bed and the blocked toilets and the white fluffy creature in the kitchen, but I decided to move with two girls and two guys into a semi-detached Victorian house in Leamington Spa, a genteel town famous for its early 19th century Regency architecture.

For all its ugliness, at least my room in the residence hall was square-shaped. One of the quirks of Britain is that designers love to add in different angles, like bay windows. There don't seem to be any right angles, which makes it tricky to fit in furniture. My room was on the ground floor, and it sucked because it was on a main street. I wedged my desk into that bay window and everyone walking past could see me, and I would watch them go by as I worked on my plastic hair tie business and occasionally on my studies.

I also knew all of the gossip of Leamington Spa.

At 2am, I would often get woken up by a conversation that might go something like this:

Loud Drunk Female Student 1: "I can't believe I kissed Fit Phil!"

Loud Drunk Female Student 2: "That's great, you've fancied him for ages!"

Loud Drunk Female Student 1: "You don't understand. About ten minutes later he went home with Big-Tits-Tina."

Loud Drunk Female Student 2: "I've always hated Big-Tits-Tina."

I heard it all.

Meanwhile in Munich, our friends Dani and Niki rented an office for New Flag that was next to a nightclub named Call Me Drella. Drella was a nickname Andy Warhol gave himself – a mixture of Cinderella and Dracula – and the club was famous for its acrobatics and the fact that you *really* needed to dress up to get in, which was convenient because when they worked late nights, they would walk from the office straight over to the club.

Dani and Niki had hired a friend of theirs, Lisa, to manage the office, write invoices and make sure everyone was getting paid, and her desk was an upturned wooden crate that had a slanting top and splinters, which got stuck in the underside of her mouse. Dani's desk looked like a massive treasure chest and was so large it had to be brought into the office on a crane that deposited it through the window. Later on, when I worked from that office, I had a desk that looked like a huge aeroplane wing.

Like many start-ups, New Flag wasn't exactly the most efficient of operations to start with. Shortly after joining, Lisa found herself alone in the office with a stack of unopened letters. She opened the first one.

New Flag GmbH
Max-Joseph-Straße 7
80333 Munich
Germany

2 October 2012

**Dear New Flag**

**Further to our final reminder letters of 2 July, 2 August and 2 September 2012, demanding your <u>overdue payment of €14</u> to be settled, we have organized for our third party debt collector to recover the outstanding amount at the date and time below.**

2 November 2012
10.00am

**Failure to comply will result in criminal proceedings.**

**Yours faithfully,**

**Munich Printers.**

Lisa looked at the time. It was 2 November 2012, and it was 9.40am. In 20 minutes' time, the debt collector would arrive. She rang Dani.

"Hi, it's Lisa."
"Oh hi! How's it going?"
"Well I opened this letter, and YOU'RE GOING TO BE ARRESTED IF YOU DON'T GET HERE IN 20 MINUTES."

It was OK, because Lisa rang the number on the letter and paid the printer the €14 (about £12.50 or $15) and no debt collector showed up, but it's the kind of thing that you have to keep an eye on when your business starts to take off because even small amounts can affect your credit rating, as we later found out. The funny thing was, the printing job was for a sign you put on your desk that read: "My favourite position is CEO." Hilarious.

In our circle of friends, Niki and Dani were known as the boys who sold plastic hairbrushes, and now they were helping us with our plastic hair bobble business too. Lisa told me that at the time, even though she thought they were kind of cool, they were definitely fugly too. The colours were horrible (Submarine Yellow was not a bestseller), and the shape was weird ("Why would you put a keychain in your hair?").

As with a lot of new trends that you think are gross to start with – think neon t-shirts, platform shoes, huge trainers – once people got used to how it looked, it started to become cool. Added to that, people were wearing invisibobbles on their wrists which, as Lisa puts it, is a very effective advertising space as people notice them.

We also had an idea for how we could make our product completely and utterly different to any other hair tie at the time, something that had never been seen before and that I felt would be fundamentally important for the success of invisibobble: our packaging.

As I've said, hair ties had been an unloved product, and we were selling our invisibobbles in those Ziploc-type clear plastic bags, which didn't look great. I knew we had to do something to make them stand out, so during the summer holidays, I had started to make little square and rectangular boxes out of cardboard, which would hold one, three, six, ten or 50 invisibobbles.

I wanted to use the cardboard boxes as a template for a clear, transparent version, with the idea being they would look cute, like candy. Just a seemingly small change to how hair ties were sold turned out to be a huge game-changer – and it's something that has helped us become profitable, iconic and recognizable now.

Our packaging helped to give invisibobble personality. We could use it to give our hair ties fun names, so instead of green, we could have 'mint to be,' or instead of pink, it could be 'blush hour,' and we could use all six sides of the cube to be creative and explain why our hair ties were different.

We also thought that we could do something fun with our displays in hair salons. One weekend when I went to visit Felix in Bath, we spent the entire time cutting out cereal packets and making them into the ideal display. We ended up with a square display with cardboard steps, on which 24 of our cute cube packs would fit, and they are almost the same design that we have today. We found our display maker online, and the first order we had was for about 300. We still work with the same guy and invisibobble has become his single largest client.

Felix and I had been approaching distributors in the UK, and we managed to get a meeting with a guy in the north of England, in a small town we'd never heard of. Distributors are absolutely crucial for companies like ours who make products, because they have networks of retailers or salons that they sell to, and getting the right distribution helps companies grow.

We got the train up north the night before our meeting and sat on the small bed in our hotel room, rehearsing what we were going to say. We had been to WHSmith and bought the fanciest fountain pen we could, thinking it would make us look more grown-up and professional than a plastic ballpoint. We imagined a *Dragon's Den* or *Shark Tank* scenario, where four business people sat in a room with excited expressions on their faces against a backdrop of exposed brickwork while we stood up, pitching our plastic hair ties. After our pitch, they would fight over who would invest.

It wasn't like that at all.

The meeting was held in a small room with no heating, and just the son of the father-and-son business turned up. However, the son seemed pretty positive about invisibobble, and eventually his dad arrived.

"Ay ya. I'm Pee-ah," he said. "Man! It's col'. I'll 'ave to sit 'ere in me cor like!"

His name was Peter, and he had to sit there in his coat, was what he meant, but the northeast accent was sometimes pretty hard for us to understand. Similar outbursts would occur throughout our presentation.

Most of the time, he didn't seem interested in us at all. I mean, why would he be, given that our product looked so strange and had a higher price-point than regular hair ties? But the more we talked, the more he realized that we'd really thought the concept through, and it would be an easy way for his sales force to make some money on the side by selling invisibobbles along with their shampoos and other hair products, known in the business as 'wet lines.' So by the end of the meeting, Pee-ah apologized about his moaning and the cold and said he thought we were really onto something. Our man and his son in the northeast signed up as our distributor for the region.

We were still 19, but we honestly looked about 15 (puberty hit kind of late), and I think our appearance sometimes made people take us less seriously. It felt ridiculous to be children presenting to grown-ups, and we thought that our age should at least start with a two, and so suddenly, we were telling people we were 22.

They wouldn't always believe us, so we had to backtrack and admit that we were still teenagers. But often people's reactions were pretty positive to start with, and some of those early relationships we still have today. The guy who makes our clear plastic packaging says he felt like we were his grandchildren when we started working together.

Even though we had our packaging, our presentation and the semblance of an office in Munich, as New Flag let us have a desk there, we were still only a few months into invisibobble (it was around autumn 2012 by now), and we were very much a scrappy start-up. Felix and I would go to meetings with distributors, place more orders with our Alibaba manufacturer and spend time sending out packs of products. Then we would both head back to university to try to catch up with our work, but realistically I'd say that at this point I spent 80% of my time on invisibobble and 20% on studying. It wasn't a great balance; in fact, it wasn't really a balance at all. I had plenty of nights where I'd wake up at 3am panicking either about an essay deadline or about whether invisibobble would grow into something and how we could make that happen.

As our products are so tiny, Dani and Niki found a space for boxes of them in their warehouse on the outskirts of Munich, and shipments from China would make their way there before being sent out to distributors by the warehouse manager for New Flag.

By the end of 2012, our first year in business, we'd made £73,000 (around $90,000) in revenue and were profitable.

We definitely weren't paying ourselves a salary, as we were reinvesting all the profits back into invisibobble to buy more stock.

The feedback on the product was still very mixed. We could have given up (and people often do) but, despite some people thinking invisibobbles were silly, we kept pushing forward.

Felix still had to trust me at this point that our hair ties had potential, because they were a female-focused product and because the hair ties themselves were my passion. But we decided to carry on, and our aim for 2013 was to go international. Whoop whoop!

# 6.
# A Water Leak In Leamington Spa

80,000 INVISIBOBBLES SOLD

**WHAT I LEARNED:**

- Vomit can set off smoke alarms
- Know your buyer: preparation is key when meeting retailers
- Starting your own business is one of the most anxiety-inducing things you can ever do

It took us a while to get the packaging right, but by March 2013, we had moved over into our cute plastic cube boxes of three, with 24 displayed on our cardboard stands in hairdressers. We sold them in Germany for €4.20 (about £3.80, or $4.60) to start with, a price we soon put up to €5 (about £4.60, or $5.50). In the UK, we sold them for £5 ($6).

Even though we had made a reasonable revenue in our first year, we were still pretty small. Through our relationship with New Flag, where we basically operated as one conjoined company, we were getting sold in hairdressers in the UK and Germany, but invisibobbles were still a niche product. We needed a retailer.

Dani and Niki had helped us with a contact at a large British pharmacy chain and they had said they were kind of interested, but they were keener on us becoming a supplier for them so they could brand our hair ties with their own label.

Own label – or private label as it's sometimes called – is when a shop makes its own version of something. So, for example, Tesco (the largest supermarket chain in Britain) sells a large bottle of Heinz tomato ketchup for around £2.80 (about $3.40), but also sells a large bottle of Tesco own-label tomato ketchup for £1 (about $1.20). Tesco is likely to have a manufacturer that makes a variety of products for its range of own-label goods, and its strategy is usually to sell them in stores at lower prices than the brand-name.

There's a lot of psychology behind this. Often people will buy the branded product, such as Heinz, over the own-label version because branded goods are perceived to be of better quality. This might be due to advertising campaigns, or because people think that branded goods like Heinz are better because they are more expensive than own-label products.

We didn't want our hair ties to become a store-brand product, something that the store would sell using their own label, stapled onto cardboard just like regular elastic hair bands. Part of the idea behind invisibobble was to completely change the hair tie category, to make it into something people were proud to buy by making it look different and packaged in a totally new way.

Everywhere we went, retailers said we were completely out of our minds to even think this product would be even remotely appropriate to sell anywhere. Why would someone spend €5 or £5 or $8 (which is how much we now sell invisibobble for in the US) for three plastic hair ties when you could easily get 20 regular elastic hair ties for €1 or £1 or $3?

Eventually, the British chain agreed to a meeting with us. To make invisibobble seem more like a proper business, we took Dani and Niki with us. We still looked like small children, but at least Dani and Niki looked like slightly older children than we did.

The head office was in a town in middle England, and many of the people living there worked for the retailer. The headquarters were pretty impressive: it was very corporate and daunting, and it made us and our products feel all the more tiny.

As we approached the reception desk, we could see the top of a computer screen and a lot of shiny dark hair drawn tightly into a large, doughnut-shaped high bun, the size of a child's football. I approached nervously and the bun moved away from the screen to reveal a round, friendly face that had clearly undergone quite a bit of decoration that morning. I said who we were, and she tapped on her computer keyboard using the longest fingernails I had ever seen.

"Have a seat, love," she said. "Your buyer will be right with you."

We sat down, feeling like the youngest and most inexperienced people there. The atmosphere was one of corporate efficiency, with women in navy-blue pencil skirts and mid-height heels meeting with salespeople from the biggest beauty manufacturers in the world. They were from companies like Procter & Gamble, which makes billion-dollar brands like Olay and Pantene, and L'Oréal, which owns everything from Maybelline to Lancôme. Most of the people waiting for meetings were middle-aged business-suit wearers from these kinds of companies, selling makeup, shampoo, toothpaste, nappies, painkillers, razors, perfume, hair dye, deodorant and all types of lotions and potions, on a massive scale.

For them, the goal was to get as many goods onto the shelves as possible, buying shelf space by the metre, with the aim of dominating that product category. If you look at the toothpaste section in any supermarket or pharmacy chain, you'll see what I mean.

Relationships with buyers at retailers are critical for brands: they are the ones who decide to sell their goods and how much shelf space to give them. If products don't sell well, buying teams can threaten to de-list them, and manufacturers might have to respond with a big advertising campaign to shift more, or reduce the price of them. Buyers have power, and meeting one from a large retailer with more than 2,000 stores in the UK was a huge deal for us.

We really stuck out, a tiny brand dressed in our cool version of smart, in blazers and dark jeans. We didn't have to wait long until our buyer, a capable woman in her 20s called Julie, came to meet us. We walked down a corridor lined with meeting rooms and she sat us down outside one of them "for a chat."

Her attitude was strict and efficient. Often at large chains the focus is on operations and making sure things get from A to B in the right quantity and at the right time, and they need to make sure their suppliers are going to be able to meet their requirements.

We tried to take all of this into account with our presentation, which was super detailed on figures. Our buyer, though rigorous, was friendly too and understood that we were a young company with a new product. She seemed positive and said she would get back to us about doing a trial run.

We went back to university feeling optimistic, but we had to knuckle down and get our academic work done. I couldn't stop thinking about whether this retailer would do a test run of invisibobble, which was exciting, but I also had books to read and management terms to understand. Some days my head would spin with the amount of work I had to do and there were very few times when I actually felt relaxed. The stress was really starting to mount.

A couple months later, during the Easter holidays, I was up a mountain in Switzerland with some university friends. We'd gone there to ski for a few days and had stopped for lunch. My phone rang, and it was Felix. "They've confirmed they want to list invisibobble!" he said.

Tears sprang to my eyes and I excused myself from the table. I walked around the corner and had a little cry. A huge, massive retailer had agreed to list invisibobble. I couldn't believe it. Then I put my sunglasses back on and went back to the group. "Did something bad happen?" one of my friends asked. "I'm fine," I said. I didn't say any more.

I didn't want to tell any of my friends about the listing for a few reasons. First, because I didn't want it to seem like I was showing off to try to get attention, that wasn't what I wanted. Also, everyone was focusing on their exams and what GPA (grade point average – it's a way of understanding how low or high you've scored in exams) they had, so talking about invisibobble didn't seem interesting or relevant and would probably result in silent responses and expressionless faces. So, it felt easier to just say nothing.

A listing confirmation is simply a statement that a retailer wants to sell your product in its stores, rather than being a detailed order. From there, we would need to negotiate how many stores invisibobble would be sold in and try to persuade them to take the maximum variety of colours. It was spring 2013, and invisibobble would arrive in stores around October, and we would be dispatching the order to the retailer around August. Up until then, we had only been sold in hairdressers, which is why getting a listing in a national UK retailer was such big news.

It was barely 15 months since the night I'd put my hair up in a telephone cord and now we might get stocked by a national retailer! But I still felt we needed to get our shit together and move up to second gear.

That turned out to be hard. I've never had a breakdown, but sometimes you get to a point in your life when the curve of anxiety shoots up and you scrape close to the edge of everything falling apart. But then you pull yourself together, and you gradually go back down the curve to normality. During my second year at university, I could feel myself climbing the curve. I would wake up at 3am and not be able to go back to sleep. Then I couldn't concentrate, I couldn't eat, and I lost weight. Anytime anyone poked me about anything I would cry, which is really not like me.

By May 2013, exams were approaching, we were doing the final negotiations with the large pharmacy chain, and we were also working with different distributors. We had two other British retailers interested and the combination of everything was getting too much.

When you start sending out orders to distributors, no news is good news. You don't get praise for what you're doing right, so silence is the best compliment. But we'd started getting complaints about quality, or that we were delivering late, and it just felt like people were saying *you're a piece of shit, your products are shit, why are they so expensive?*

It's very different delivering late to a large distributor than to one hairdresser who makes an order online, because the worst case scenario is you get one angry customer. With a distribution company, it's like *what the fuck are you doing?* And in our case, they were a million times bigger than we were.

But we did mess up. We'd risen from nothing to getting distributors on board and a listing at a national retailer, pretty much by ourselves, but the further you rise, the further you have to fall. As much as we were learning loads and having fun, we were almost constantly worried. It was like a rollercoaster: we'd have massive highs when we found a new distributor or had a retailer interested, and then there were constant lows when we plunged back down after something went wrong in the business.

One day I reached what I think must have been the ultimate low point I had at university. I was at the campus library, trying to work, but I couldn't because I had so much anxiety running through my veins. I'd had one of my 3am wake-ups and even though I'd been up for hours, I hadn't felt hungry. I felt the stress physically: I could feel it in my knees especially, and I had to keep standing up and shake my legs out to take the feeling away. I went into the stairwell of the library, sat down and called Felix.

"I … I … I … I … c … c … can't do this anymore," I sobbed. It was the kind of crying where your face goes really ugly and you can't breathe. I was distraught.

"You can. You suck it up, you have an exam, just like everyone else. And you're just going to get through it."

That wasn't what I needed to hear.

"Fuck you." I hung up.

I couldn't stop crying. It was the kind of sobbing where your shoulders are heaving and your face is screwed up and red, as if your body is trying to expel something. My face was the definition of ugly crying, and I had to drag myself through campus to the bus stop, ugly crying. I had to sit and wait for the bus, still ugly crying. Then I sat on the bus for half an hour, ugly crying. Finally, I reached my shitty room in my shitty house where I could continue my ugly crying in peace.

I'd say I was so anxious that I scraped the edge of a breakdown for a good month during the end of that second university year.

But even though Felix was sometimes tough, I couldn't have started the business without him. To go through something like that completely on my own would have been impossible, because at university I felt totally by myself. No one understood what I was going through and people would often make fun of invisibobble. "Haha, it's a hair tie, how stressful could it possibly be?" Even when it started appearing in big retail chains their response would be: "Oh, so you've made the product and it's in the shops, so what is there left to do?" Now people understand a bit better that invisibobble is my life and it's what I do all day, every day, although until recently, people would still ask, "Is that your full-time job?"

But Felix and I complemented each other because his course had many more assignments than mine, so for a few days each month he'd be working solidly, while I took over invisibobble. For me, my course was more like nothing, nothing, nothing, and then DIE, where I'd need several weeks out of the business to concentrate on my studies.

It was toward the end of our second year at university, and we all had exams. Felix and I were also in the middle of negotiating how much the pharmacy chain would order, and they eventually agreed to selling invisibobble in four colours – black, brown, white and blue – in 250 stores. We were ecstatic but also super stressed because we'd had to revise while still negotiating and this involved several trips to middle England during the university term. There was a lot of administration involved, and one of the forms we had to fill in concerned New Flag's credit rating. (At this point, New Flag owned 50% of invisibobble and therefore paperwork included the name New Flag, since we decided it would be the outward-facing company when dealing with partners). I called Niki to ask for it.

"No," Niki's said down the line.
"Why not?"
"We cannot let them run a credit check. It won't work."

"What?"

"Well, there's this invoice we forgot to pay last year …"

"What invoice? How much for?"

"€14."

I didn't for one moment imagine that there would be a problem with the credit rating, but remember that letter Lisa opened back in October 2012 demanding an overdue payment of €14? No one had told me or Felix anything about it because they didn't realize it would be an issue, but it had turned into a massive problem.

That one missed €14 payment for New Flag to print the words "My favourite position is CEO" onto a nameplate had given them a poor credit rating, and even though they'd eventually paid it, the black mark was still against them. We literally had to get a lawyer involved to sort it out. Can you imagine being a lawyer who has spent ages training and years dealing with big contracts and then a small company like ours turns up and asks you to sort out a €14 invoice?

I couldn't lie on the form, so I had to say that New Flag had a poor credit rating, and then I rang the pharmacy chain to explain what had happened. Luckily, they were OK with it. I had no idea, but these seemingly small admin issues really mattered, and having a poor credit rating causes start-ups to fail. Often, founders are focused on more 'exciting' things, like getting new customers, but you also have to ruthlessly focus on the admin side. As I said before, the devil really is in the details.

Not only would I get woken up by the staggering-home students of Leamington Spa going past my ground floor bedroom with the paper-thin windows, but my own housemates would also go out drinking a lot.

Having missed so many lectures and seminars, I had a lot of catching up to do and was feeling pretty stressed. Two of my housemates finished all of their exams a day earlier than me, and I'd begged them to keep quiet when they got home from celebrating, as I was still revising and would need a good night's sleep.

My room was right by the front door and it was also close to the kitchen, where we'd often have after-parties. I went to bed early and put my earplugs in, just in case.

At 6am, the smoke detector went off.

I got up, went to my bedroom door and opened it. My housemate Tim was standing there, holding a daisy.

"I have a flower for you," he said, handing it to me, standing diagonally in my doorway.

"Tim, this isn't funny. I have an exam today. I asked you to be quiet. Fuck off!" I shouted, my hands over my ears from the screaming smoke alarm.

The alarm carried on blasting, but there was no smoke anywhere. Instead, water started streaming out of it, and Tim, in his drunken state, grabbed the smoke detector and ripped the whole thing out of the ceiling. The water didn't stop, and there's a bathroom upstairs, so I ran up to see if someone had left the shower on or if it was overflowing.

The shower was fine, but there was the smell of alcoholic sick in the bathroom. Turns out that Charlotte, one of my other housemates, had also finished her exams the day before and had woken up in the night feeling sick after an evening of celebrating. She hadn't made it to the toilet so had vomited in her sink, putting the taps on full-blast so it didn't block the plughole.

But instead, everything had overflowed, and the liquid had made its way through the ceiling and down into the smoke alarm, meaning that at 6am on the morning of my final exam I had to navigate vomit water in our hallway and two useless drunken housemates.

This was the kind of thing that happened all the time, and it was quite a contrast to the corporate meetings I was going to for invisibobble where I was sometimes pretending to be a super mature 22-year-old with an international brand of hair ties. The reality was, I was dealing with vomit water, treading a fine balance with my lectures and seminars and trying to ward off a nervous breakdown.

It took about a month after I finished my second-year exams for the anxiety curve to subside, and that summer, Felix and I had another project to get worried about: the pallet.

# 7.
# The Pallet on the Pavement

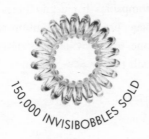

150,000 INVISIBOBBLES SOLD

**WHAT I LEARNED:**

- Retail distribution and delivery is super detailed, super important and super difficult for teenagers, or anyone
- There are millions of shipping acronyms and the Urban Dictionary is no help
- Reading and understanding customers' instructions properly is vital to avoid fines

Eventually, after all our negotiations, we got an email from the British pharmacy chain confirming their order, which was one pallet of invisibobbles.

If you don't know what a pallet is, well, neither did we. It turns out, it's a base on which you put your boxes of products so they can be transported safely. They're made from several parallel pieces of wood or plastic, supported by three thicker pieces underneath. They're roughly square-shaped and about eight inches deep and are made in a very particular way so that forklift trucks can pick them up and move them around warehouses. You pack your products on top of these pallets to precise measurements so they can fit on forklift trucks, into lorries, and onto shelves at warehouses.

Pallets are, in fact, a big thing. There is an entire industry around them, with whole companies that just do things with pallets. They make, repair, manage, procure, recondition and recycle them, produce bespoke ones and provide pallet procurement services.

There's not much that is funny about pallets, but I wish there was.

Pallets have a relatively simple construction, but there are about 20 different shapes and sizes, which to the regular person look very similar. Retailers work with different types of pallets, so you have to make sure you get the right ones and you can get fined for getting any number of things wrong, as we found out. You never know what you're going to have to end up doing when you start a company, but 'pallet packing expert' isn't something I thought I'd be adding to my CV.

The retailer had ordered one pallet, and it was up to us to fit as many boxes of invisibobble hair ties on to it as we possibly could, seal it and send it off. Simple. We were delighted with the order, of course, but then the emails started, and the endless forms to fill in, with things that looked something like this:

*MOQ*
*Inner quantity*
*Outer quantity*
*Pallet type*
*EAN*

Then there was a line of three-letter acronyms.

*EXW / FCA / FAS / FOB / CFR / CIF / CPT / CIP / OAF /*
*DDU / DDP / DES / DEQ / – mark as appropriate*

*LOL. OMG. WTF?!*

We started Googling.

*EXW = Ex Wife*
*FCA = Fat Chick Attitude*
*FAS = To Fail*

Although they were funny, the Urban Dictionary's suggestions weren't much help, as surely a 'fat chick attitude' pallet wasn't an option, so we spent a lot of time deciphering all the acronyms via Wikipedia and an online glossary. Those three-letter acronyms are shipping terms referring to who is responsible for what, and at what point goods become the responsibility of the buyer.

Inner and outer refers to the number of packs per small box and then the number of small boxes per larger box and EAN means European Article Number, which relates to the bar code.

We hadn't needed to fill out forms like this before, because the hairdressers we were supplying didn't need barcodes or tracking, whereas with retailers everything needs to be documented with barcodes so they can monitor how much stock they have.

Getting all the shipping information right was, and still is, critical for getting our tiny packs of invisibobbles from the factory in China onto the right ship (at that point we were still flying our products over), delivered to the right European port and onto the right lorry to the right distribution centre at the right time. Packages have to be the right size and weight and with the right labels to get where they need to go. Everything has to be exact.

Right. So, we found a pallet supplier on Amazon and had one delivered to Felix's parents' home in Munich, where we'd headed for the summer holidays (since the 'warehouse' was a small room that did not allow for pallets to be assembled). Before we could fill it up, we had to put our invisibobbles into their cute, clear plastic box packaging, three per pack. Nowadays our packaging has changed slightly, which means a machine can pack it, but back then our packs arrived flat. Felix and I would play a game, trying to erect the flat, crash-lock boxes and then pack invisibobbles into as many boxes as we could in a given time. Felix would win most of the time, but I wasn't really bothered, as it was just a fun way of getting a very rudimentary task done.

We took the pallet down to the basement and had a lot of fun fitting our tiny packs of three invisibobbles into boxes and then on to the pallet, making sure there were a mixture of colours per tier. When we'd finished stacking the boxes carefully, it was almost more than six feet high and just over three feet across.

Not only did we have to fit as many packs as we could on to that first pallet, but we had to wrap it carefully so it reached its destination full and intact. Usually, there's an industrial cling-film machine that would do this in a warehouse, but we didn't have that luxury so we cling-filmed it carefully ourselves, using packets we'd bought at the supermarket. Packing that pallet was the activity of the day, and we congratulated ourselves that we'd done it.

Then Felix's dad came down to the basement.

"We just finished our first-ever pallet!" Felix said.
"How are you going to get that out of here?"
"Huh?"
"It's a lot bigger than when you brought just the pallet in."

We'd carried the empty plastic pallet sideways down into the basement, but now it was full, it definitely wouldn't fit back up the stairs and through the door.

"How many packs are in there?" Felix's dad said.

There were 19,200 three-packs, which meant there were exactly 57,600 invisibobble hair ties in our pallet.

*Well, fuck.*

I think this was the moment in the history of the company where I felt the stupidest. Perhaps in my whole life. We had to unroll the cling-film and unpack the entire 19,200 packs in the basement, and then transport everything to on the pavement outside the front of the house, because otherwise we wouldn't have been able to get the full pallet through the door. Luckily, it was a nice day and doing it the second time was quicker. When we were done we sat there waiting for the truck we'd organized to come and pick it up. It arrived, picked up our precious pallet with a forklift and drove off.

Our 19,200 invisibobble packs were on their way to be sold in one of the largest retailers in the UK.

It felt a bit like when you've packed a suitcase full of all your favourite things to go on holiday and you say goodbye to it on the conveyor belt at the airport, hoping it's not goodbye forever and that it will arrive intact at the other end. Each of the 57,600 hair ties felt like a little baby to us and all we could do was hope it would survive the journey from Munich to a distribution centre somewhere on the island that is Great Britain. Western civilization could surely safely transport our 19,200 babies across the channel.

A couple days later we got an email.

From: Logistics Team
To: invisibobble
Sent: Thu, 11 July 2013, 12.53 PM
Subject: Delivery Rejection

**This is an auto-generated notification that the following goods delivery has been rejected.**

**Ref: INVISI-BT124567AJ**

**Invisibobble: Mixed assortment**

**Units: 19,200**

**Details: Missed delivery time**

**Contact Delivery Services on 0330 184 576 quoting the reference number above.**

**Do not reply to this email. The mailbox is unmonitored.**

Our delivery had been refused.

Our 19,200 packets of invisibobbles, 57,600 hair ties, which would retail for a total of £96,000 (about $118,000), had been rejected.

It turns out that we had booked the wrong kind of logistics company to deliver our pallet. There's a big difference between firms that can deliver on a particular day, and those that can deliver within a particular 30-minute timeslot, which is what the retailer required.

I called the number on the email and was in a queue for about 20 minutes, listening to jolly hold music that repeated over and over again, sitting on speaker phone with Felix, Dani and Niki in their office in Munich next to the nightclub, panicking and wondering where on earth our precious 19,200 packets of invisibobbles had gone.

An efficient British female voice answered and told us that obviously we should have booked a very specific logistics company that could deliver at a very specific time. We rearranged the delivery and our pallet arrived safely at last.

But two weeks later, we got another email.

"You fucked up your pallet delivery and these are your shitty fines," went the subject line, or something a bit less sweary.

Even though our 57,600 invisibobbles had arrived OK and we thought we'd done everything right apart from timing (there was a manual about delivery, and we had spent two weeks reading it), we got fined.

We got fined because we filled in our pallet form with blue ink instead of black, and scanners cannot read blue ink, so an actual person had to read the form.

Also, we got fined even more because there has to be a precise gap of 0.79 inches from the edge of the box of invisibobbles to the edge of the pallet and ours was 0.59 inches. We also got fined because we delivered our pallet at one minute past our 30-minute delivery slot. We got fined because we used plastic tape instead of paper tape to seal the larger boxes, and we got fined because we packed the pallet slightly wrong and the forklift truck couldn't pick it up in the distribution centre.

As 19 year olds, we didn't really get it. But these kinds of logistics operations are very precise because they receive things into the warehouses and send them out to shops all over the country and everything has to happen smoothly for shops to get deliveries, shelves to be full and people to be able to buy stuff. If anything messes up that process and a human being has to get involved, things get slower and time is money. Hence the fines.

Logistics is serious stuff, and we were learning it the hard way. (It wasn't always us that messed up the deliveries.

One time a truck driver was running late, and because he knew he was going to miss the delivery slot, he dumped two or three pallets full of our invisibobbles by the side of the road when it was raining, and the cardboard cartons fell apart. That was the logistics company's fault, so we got refunded.)

At one point, I didn't think I would ever see invisibobbles in the shops at all because of all the pallet palaver. But we paid the fines (they cost us a few hundred euros) and by October that year, I saw our first invisibobbles in a real shop, just around the corner from my poorly constructed student home in Leamington Spa. Getting into that particular retailer is like a rite of passage, because they have a reputation for only selling good-quality items, and we were delighted to get that first test run.

# 8.
# Fifty Shades of Pink

200,000 INVISIBOBBLES SOLD

**WHAT I LEARNED:**

- Always, always double check and confirm details in writing with manufacturers
- Pretty in pink is not so pretty in murky white
- You have to put the brand first, even if it means fights later

What cost us a lot more than a few hundred euros in 2013 is what I'll call 'Fifty Shades of Pink.' Back then, our invisibobbles were only available in bright primary colours (we had reduced the selection down to six from 27) and they had been selling fine. But our distributors kept asking if we had pink invisibobbles, and I could see that it would be a good colour to have. So, we ordered several thousand pink invisibobbles from our manufacturer (we originally called them 'Candy Pink'), sent them out to our distributors and waited for them to sell out and for the reorders to roll in.

But one day I got a text from a hairdresser in Germany, with a picture of a kind of weird, off-white invisibobble, saying that the day before, it had been pink. *The day before, it had been pink??*

Then other people started complaining about them too, posting photos on Instagram, which is never good when you fuck up. It was my uni summer holidays, and I was in the Munich office with Felix, Dani, Niki and Lisa, and all hell broke loose. We had spent a lot of money getting these new, in-demand pink invisibobbles, and now, somehow, there were white invisibobbles in the mix, something we definitely hadn't ordered. We were trying to find out what had gone wrong – maybe the factory had sent us undyed invisibobbles by mistake or maybe they had got wet somehow. We spent ages unpacking boxes, calling our warehouse, ringing distributors and scouring social media to see if there were any more complaints.

Lisa had put some pink invisibobbles on the windowsill in the office. There was no air conditioning, the windows didn't open and there were no blinds. It was boiling hot, and Lisa would pile empty boxes on top of each other as high up the windows as possible to block out the burning sunshine, so there was very little room for anything else. Anyway, about a half hour later, we realized the pink invisibobbles had gone different shades of pale. They were being bleached by the sun's UV rays.

*How did this even happen?* I thought. *We are going to have to recall all of these faded, weird invisibobbles before any more get out.*

We emailed the manufacturer, who simply replied that yes, indeed, pink is an unstable colour that reacts with UV rays, but because we hadn't requested to add UV protection, he just went ahead and didn't. *Of course.*

If our pink invisibobbles were going white within 30 minutes of being exposed to the sunshine in Germany, where there is limited sunshine, what the hell would happen to them in sunny places like Spain or Portugal, where by then we had distributors who were also supplying them to hair salons? We had to call everyone and tell them to stop sending out the products, ask salons to return them, and reply to every complaint that came through on Facebook, Instagram and via email. Then we got the manufacturer to make proper pink invisibobbles, with UV protection, and send them out again. It was a nightmare that took about a month to sort out and was definitely our biggest issue that year. I think it cost more than $30,000 to fix (about £25,000), which was a massive chunk of our revenue.

Around the same time we started making pink invisibobbles, I also decided we should produce a completely transparent version. That would fit in very well with the whole 'invisible' part of the invisibobble. They don't leave a dent your hair, and a clear version would look cool and almost invisible too. I wanted to call it 'Crystal Clear,' but Felix, Dani and Niki were really against the idea to start with. They thought it would look like a strange piece of plastic, plus a total of eight hair tie colours was still too many, they thought. The bigger your assortment, the more expensive it is to produce and the more pressure there is to sell everything you've made.

But I was insistent that clear would work, because it's neutral and would match any hair colour, plus it looked different to anything already on the market. It was impossible to get clear fabric-covered elastic hair ties, and I also figured it would be a talking point when people wore invisibobbles around their wrists.

It turned out that Crystal Clear became an instant bestseller, and it hasn't left the podium since then. True Black and Pretzel Brown came next, and then Blush Hour pink, after we got the pink colour right. Choosing fun colour names also helped to give invisibobble personality.

One thing, though, is how important it is that we sell three invisibobbles of the same colour in one pack.

For me, doing so looks clean and helps the product become iconic. It's like if you mix up different candies, one of the flavours always gets left. I hate orange-flavoured sweets, and if I see a mixed pack with orange in it, I get put off buying it. I love Lindt chocolate balls (real name: Lindor chocolate truffles) because you can buy a whole box of the same flavour without having to worry about the ones you don't like.

I think it's the same with invisibobble. If we mixed the colours, the packs would start looking cheap, and there's a risk that people wouldn't buy them because they didn't like one of the shades. Keeping three of the same colour together also means our packs have personality and we can create limited-edition colours. So, we've had 'Hawkwardly Good Looking,' a mint green 'feathered friend' invisibobble, which was part of our Circus Collection in 2017. That also included a blue invisibobble we called 'Bad Hair Day? Irrelephant,' with a cute elephant on the pack. On Valentine's Day we've added phrases like "Roses are red, violets are blue, invisibobbles cost less than dinner for two."

We also know that people tend to keep hair ties in different places: one in their hair, one in their handbag, and one on their desk at work, let's say. So, three is a kind of practical number for someone to buy, too.

Whether we can mix up colours in a pack is an argument I have since had with our sales teams, because retailers are constantly asking for us to do so. But I have the long-term health of the brand at heart, and I know it wouldn't be right.

We had an ambition to be the go-to hair accessories brand, and that started with reinventing hair ties. Instead of people seeing them as a commodity, where they buy 50 at a time, we've tried to make something that people can use over and over again (an invisibobble will go back to its original size if you put it in hot water), a product that is lovable as well as functional. They are made of plastic, which is fully recyclable, unlike regular elastic hair ties that often have a metal bar holding them together, making them harder to recycle.

# 9.
# The Great Hair Bobble Hack

450,000 INVISIBOBBLES SOLD

**WHAT I LEARNED:**

- **Personalizing letters and emails to journalists and bloggers really works**
- **We had no experience. We didn't know the rules and we broke them in the cheekiest ways**
- **Retailer negotiations can feel like a game**

We knew that as well as being a cool hair accessory that didn't give you a headache, invisibobble was also fashionable and looked very different to anything that had been around before.

Back in Munich, Lisa had taken on marketing for invisibobble (as well as doing admin for New Flag) and put together a list of all the important and relevant journalists in the UK and Germany and sent personalized packets of invisibobbles to them all. She would find pictures of each person and print them out, then pick hair ties in colours that matched their outfits and send them with individual letters. I loved this attention to detail.

Then she would stalk the journalists. She would call every single one of them, which she said was a "huge pain," but it worked. About 80% of them were happy to take her call, and about 50% ended up writing about invisibobble. That was huge.

In 2013, Instagram and YouTube hadn't properly taken off as being an influencer wasn't really a thing yet, but blogs were, especially in the UK. Lisa had sent some invisibobbles to a woman called Jane Cunningham, known as the British Beauty Blogger, and she had reviewed them on her website, calling them "the handiest thing you'll find for your hair this summer," with a picture of two bright red hair ties.

The British Beauty Blogger has a background in beauty journalism, and she's quite investigative and trusted, and retailers looked to well-known bloggers to pick up on trends early. At 11.40am on 11 July 2013, just after the British Beauty Blogger had written her piece about invisibobble, we got a short email from a well-known fashion retailer:

From: "Michelle Goldstein"
To: support@invisibobble.com
Sent: Thu, 11 July 2013, 11:40 AM GMT+02:00
Subject: Listing invisibobble

**Good morning**

**We are very keen to stock your product – please can someone get in touch?**

**Thanks**

**Michelle Goldstein
Assistant Buyer – Beauty**

This retailer had about 300 stores in the UK, with a head office in London, and I could not believe they had contacted us. Even though it was a smaller chain, being stocked there would help to take our hair ties from being seen as functional to being seen as fashionable. It was also a place where I loved to shop, so them wanting to stock invisibobble felt like the biggest compliment ever.

The slight problem was that when we got the email, Felix and I weren't in the UK. We were in Amsterdam, casually walking along a footpath beside a canal after celebrating his mum's birthday. As we know, Felix loves details and would check his BlackBerry every two minutes, so within seconds of Michelle hitting send, we were jumping up and down on a cobbled street whooping and cheering.

We stood by the canal and wrote back to Michelle and organized to go and meet her in London. And then we went back to the hotel in Amsterdam to prepare for the meeting. We carefully adapted the presentation we had given to the large pharmacy chain, called Lisa in the office in Munich to get her to print out copies in colour and bind them professionally with proper clear-plastic covers. We asked Lisa to include invisibobble samples and our business cards before couriering everything to us in Amsterdam, ready for the last-minute flight we had booked to London.

But the package didn't arrive in time.

We had no choice but to leave the hotel to get our flight for the meeting the next day, practising who was going to say what and memorizing all our figures and business projections, always bearing in mind the kind of person who shopped at the store: fashionable teenagers. We would have to post our presentation to Michelle as a follow-up, and we hoped and prayed that our enthusiasm would get us through the meeting.

Before the meeting, Felix and I had looked up the buyer and saw that she was a young woman, which was good because she would be in our target audience.

One of the worst things we found in those early days was if we had an older male buyer, as they are much harder to sell to. They would study us analytically, and if we didn't have prior sales or were launching a new product, they would be much more risk averse. So when we saw this young, fashionable-looking woman's picture, we were super happy. Felix was even happier because she happened to be very attractive.

The fashion brand was part of a bigger group and the reception area was full of people wheeling big suitcases and rails of clothes around, and it felt pretty young and fashionable. Felix's mouth dropped open when Michelle approached us because she was wearing one of those very tight, Herve Leger-style bandage dresses, which was cut low and showed off a lot of cleavage, which she'd paired with high heels and groomed hair; kind of a big show outfit.

I was nervous but tried to be cool, and Felix was trying to get his jaw off the floor as she sat us down in a meeting room.

"Cute product," Michelle said.

I took a deep breath, all ready for my performance, where I'd tell Michelle how I'd invented invisibobble, how it eased my headaches and how we knew our customers loved to wear it on their wrists because it looked cool. Then it would be Felix's turn to talk about numbers.

But within about three minutes she said:

"Thanks. What's your retail price?"

Before Felix told her, he started to launch into our sales figures and how, even though he's a guy, he still got how cool invisibobble was, and how guys still discussed our spiral hair ties when they saw them on girls' wrists, and even though we were a small company, our operations were slick, and why she should …

"Sure. What's your MOQ?"

MOQ is minimum order quantity, and if someone's asking you for that, it means they want to place an order.

Felix and I had tried to stage this big performance with our nonexistent presentation, but here we were, five minutes into a meeting with the UK's most fashionable store, with Michelle the hot buyer asking for our MOQ. Eight minutes after we sat down in the meeting room, she ordered 1,000 packs, and then she was thanking us and waving us to the lift. Whoop! We high-fived. Three thousand invisibobbles sold in eight minutes.

It was clear that Michelle had been hired because she had a good feeling for what customers liked and her job was to find the hottest trends that would be tried out in the company's flagship stores. It was a very different meeting to the one we had with the large British pharmacy chain, because Michelle based her decisions on how she felt about the product and moved much more quickly.

We'd arrived at the meeting very prepared, with our presentation and numbers all ready, but we learned that if someone emails saying, "Hi we want to stock your product," it means they want to stock your product. The sale is in the bag, so the best thing we could have done would be to focus on fulfilling the order and filling out all that endless paperwork.

This time, we didn't need to pack a pallet. Instead, we needed to learn all about cardboard boxes. It was relatively straightforward, but the retailer had a 'no sharp objects' policy in its warehouse, which meant we had to order special boxes that would be sealed with paper tape that could be opened without using a knife or scissors.

By October 2013, invisibobbles were being sold in three British retailers: one that gave us kind of a sense of verification that our product worked, another that gave us the approval that we were cool, and a third, smaller chain that had approached us, making us know we were wanted.

We also had a breakthrough in Germany with a new way of selling beauty products: a company that sent boxes of new makeup, skincare and hair products to people who paid a subscription fee each month. It had been founded in Berlin in 2011, the same year as invisibobble. The kinds of people who were happy to pay for the subscription boxes were people who loved new stuff, or early adopters. Now it's massive, but back then it was pretty small, with around 16,000 subscribers, and it was super cool.

Lisa and I really wanted to get invisibobble into these boxes. And because the hair ties are obviously something you wear, unlike a shampoo, say, people could see them and talk about them. We thought that the boxes would be ideal for us, and we wanted to send them 16,000 individual hair ties, which would be sent out to 16,000 hip, young people, exactly the audience we wanted to reach.

The makers of hair and skincare products would provide their shampoos and moisturizers for free and in return they would get their products into the hands of trendsetters. They would also get feedback, so it was a bit like a new way of doing market research.

But Dani and Niki thought we had gone nuts.

They thought we were crazy because of the investment we wanted to make, which would be several thousand euros, a huge amount for us (Felix and I were only 20 years old), and they really fought it.

In the end, Felix was the one who really went for it, which was very unlike him at the time. He's the one who doesn't want to spend money on anything, you know, *do we really need electricity?*, that kind of thing, and I think we would be broke by now if not for him because we would have invested in everything we weren't sure about. But the beauty boxes felt like the right kind of thing to do, and they were.

Suddenly, invisibobble was everywhere. Everywhere, but not in German retailers. Yet.

Some months before, Dani and Niki had got a meeting with an upmarket German beauty retailer, and they were trying to sell them Tangle Teezer. The retailer was interested, but the price they wanted to pay was far too low, so Dani and Niki turned it down. They went to more mass-market retailers instead and got Tangle Teezer listed in over 2,000 store doors.

One day, they got an email from the upmarket chain, with the subject line: "Just give us the stupid plastic hairbrush!" Those weren't the exact words, but they asked for a presentation, detailing the different colours and sizes Tangle Teezer came in, with a view to placing an order.

Retailers are very competitive, and if they see that all their rivals are stocking a particular product they will want it as well, because if you don't sell that product it's just embarrassing. Lisa wrote back, asking if they would also be interested in seeing our new product, invisibobble. No, came the answer.

Lisa carefully put a PowerPoint presentation together, branding each slide with the Tangle Teezer logo. About halfway through, still under the Tangle Teezer heading, she included pictures of invisibobbles (ignoring that they'd said they weren't interested), in their cute colours and packaging, explaining our unique selling points such as traceless and kind to hair.

She got an email back, stating they would like to order Tangle Teezers, but saying nothing at all about invisibobble. When it came to filling out the relevant forms for the posh German retailer to stock Tangle Teezer, Lisa had an idea. What if she just quietly added invisibobble to the listing?

There are various bits of boring information you have to fill in on listing forms, including names and colours, how much products weigh, what materials they are made of and the EAN code, which forms part of the barcode.

Lisa filled out all of these details for each type of Tangle Teezer (also known as a product reference), with the product description looking something like this:

| Tangle Teezer | The Original | Purple Electric | 50 grams |
|---|---|---|---|
| Tangle Teezer | The Original | Coral Glory | 50 grams |
| Tangle Teezer | Company Styler | Black Gloss | 100 grams |

But then, being Lisa, she thought: *They said no invisibobbles, well, ha, they are going to get some invisibobbles!*

So she included this too:

| Tangle Teezer | invisibobble | Submarine Yellow | 10 grams |
|---|---|---|---|
| Tangle Teezer | invisibobble | Navy Blue | 10 grams |

She snuck invisibobble onto the form, making it seem as if they were a type of Tangle Teezer, just like The Original and The Wet Detangler were.

We all held our breath for a few weeks.

Would anyone from the posh store notice that the invisibobble product they had said they weren't interested in had magically appeared on their forms?

But then the purchase order came. Along with several thousand Tangle Teezer Originals and Tangle Teezer Wet Detanglers, they had also ordered several thousand packs of Tangle Teezer invisibobble! This kind of reminded me of my sister Louise. When she was about four years old, she refused to eat anything that wasn't chicken. The solution? My parents just told her all food is chicken, and she was a happy chap.

At the time, buyers in the head office would decide which products they wanted to stock and would add them to a computer system. Then individual store managers would make their own orders from that system based on what their customers wanted. For example, if it was a store in a small village, they might see that people didn't wear a lot of makeup around there, so they'd order more face creams than lipsticks.

With invisibobble being distributed in the subscription boxes and being written about in the press, store managers started to hear about them and would simply type invisibobble into their ordering system. Because we had snuck it onto the listing, it appeared in the system and they could order it. And because sales ended up being great, no one from the buying team seemed to notice. Our great hair bobble hack had worked!

It didn't end there. In stores, every square inch is accounted for, so a reason buyers sometimes give for not listing something is because they simply don't have room. This was the case with a large, mainstream pharmacy chain in Germany, but instead of giving up when they said no, we tried another great hair bobble hack. We noticed that their hair dryers were displayed lengthways on a top shelf near hair accessories, and we asked if they could display them widthways instead, so the narrower side of the box faced out and there would be room for our invisibobble display. To cut a long story short, they said yes, and we are now listed in all of their 2,000 stores.

Lisa was the queen of the hair bobble hacks. We had very little budget for marketing, so she had to mine her contacts and think creatively about how to get invisibobble out there.

She was friends with Niki's girlfriend at the time, Talia, who was a model. Talia had a fashion blog around 2013 when they were just starting to be a thing, before Instagram really took off, and she was pretty influential. Talia got invited to Paris Fashion Week and Lisa went with her from Munich for a fun weekend. Paris Fashion Week happens twice a year and is one of the biggest events for the industry, where the world's most high-end designers show their collections.

And of course, Lisa took invisibobbles with her: she'd made a special sticker, reading "Fashion Week Edition," and stuck these on about 300 packs. They got to Paris and turned up at the venue super early and managed to get past security together, just acting as if they belonged there and had a job to do before the show started. Lisa's attitude was, well, if she got caught, so what? She wouldn't be coming back anyway.

Lisa snuck in, and before anyone could stop her, she got out her special edition packs of invisibobbles and put them into every single goody bag on every single chair in the front row. And those chairs would soon hold the butts of some of the most influential fashion journalists and celebrities in the world. Then she handed out packs after the show had finished, just acting as if she was an official promotional person.

After that, we scoured blogs, live streams and magazines to see if we could spot our hair ties on anyone's wrists or in their hair, and when we found a few, Lisa would make the pictures into a collage and send them as part of our PR to other journalists and editors. She would also send invisibobble to TV producers, talent agencies and modelling agencies and relentlessly call and follow-up with them to see if any of their clients would be wearing our hair ties. Over time, we spotted them on Cara Delevingne and Candice Swanepoel, and we even saw Khloe Kardashian wearing an invisibobble in an episode of *Keeping Up With the Kardashians*. Clearly, keeping up now included wearing an invisibobble.

# 10.

# The Mercedes
# and the Intern

1 MILLION INVISIBOBBLES SOLD

**WHAT I LEARNED:**

- **Never assume perception equals reality**
- **Ten grand in cash does indeed fit into a suitcase**
- **Sometimes you have to go with your gut instinct about new versions of your product**

Halfway through 2013, less than two years since we started the business, invisibobble was being sold in five or six European countries, and we were on track to be in 12 countries by the end of that year.

That sounds unbelievable, but it really was because we were in this weird segment of the hair accessories industry that we had invented for ourselves. We were able to get into hair salons because we had a new type of product that didn't clash with the exclusivity deals they had with shampoo suppliers, and it was easy for distributors to add invisibobble to their range of goods because it was so small and light. Easy to sell, easy to buy.

We were also able to get into pharmacies, because it was around the time that they had opened up to selling things other than medicine. Portuguese pharmacies, for example, had previously been a place people would go to for medical expertise, and that started with pharmacists selling prescription drugs and extended to them stocking creams and lotions that would deal with particular skin problems, for example. If you needed sunscreen, you would ask your local pharmacist for advice; they were the experts.

But with the rise of supermarkets selling lotions and potions as well as food and drink, pharmacists had competition and became more open to stocking other types of products. They were realizing that if a woman went in to buy headache pills, maybe she could also do with an anti-headache hair tie. It was astonishing how much we were selling in such a small country as Portugal, and it seemed that everyone we knew who went on holiday there came back and would say, "Wow, Portugal has been invisibobblified."

When people buy hair products, they are usually very particular, which is why there are shampoos for every kind of hair you can possibly imagine. Long hair, short hair, dyed hair, blonde hair, grey hair, fine hair, thirsty hair, hungry hair, floppy hair, hair that feels happy, hair that feels sad, even hair that wants to feel ecstatic when it's washed in a waterfall – you know the kind of hair I mean.

But we were discovering that people with all types of hair liked invisibobble. Some were choosing it because it looked cool, some because they liked not getting a ponytail dent, and others because invisibobble solved the headache problem, like me.

We had made contact with a Polish distributor, two guys who had agreed to drive to Munich from Warsaw, which is about an eight-hour drive. It's pretty far, but they were keen to come over because they had a Mercedes, which to them was A Big Deal, because it's a German-engineered car and they wanted to get it serviced at a German garage.

Felix had been emailing and phoning the two guys, and it all seemed very positive. In fact it was so positive, they said they wanted to buy €10,000 (about $11,000) worth of our invisibobbles and they were bringing €10,000 in cash. I was gutted I couldn't be there, because I wanted to see what €10,000 in notes actually looked like. I mean, could it fit in a briefcase, or would it all be packed in black plastic sacks in the back of their Mercedes?

Felix had organized to meet them in the Munich office with the treasure chest desk and the aeroplane wing, and he was super excited because he'd been negotiating with them and they said they would be bringing these wads of cash. He was alone in the office when the two guys arrived, one tall and thin in a leather jacket and suit trousers, and the other shorter and rotund in a shirt and jeans.

He made the two guys a coffee and sat down with them at one end of the small office, around the only normal-looking table we had. Having learned from our fashion retailer that if someone says they are ready to buy it usually means they are, Felix was ready for an easy meeting. He'd also been wondering what €10,000 looks like and was glancing around for either a briefcase or some lumpy plastic sacks, but before he could start the meeting, the taller guy said something in Polish to the shorter guy, and the shorter guy turned to Felix and said, "We need to re-park our Mercedes. We don't think it's on a good street."

Felix thought this was a bit odd but offered to help them find a better parking space. They said they were fine and left. Their two coffees, untouched, sat at the table for 20 minutes. Then 40 minutes. Felix called the shorter guy, but no answer. He left a voicemail: "Can I help you with parking, is everything OK?" He tried the taller guy, but still no answer.

The two Polish guys didn't come back.

Not only did they not come back, but Felix then called and emailed every day for two weeks. I yelled, "How could you fuck this up so badly? They had TEN THOUSAND EUROS IN CASH!!!!"

It took two weeks for the shorter guy to eventually answer his phone. The conversation went something like this:

Felix: "What happened? You came all the way from Warsaw and disappeared!"

Shorter guy: "We thought what you did was so rude."

Felix: "What?"

Shorter guy: "We drove all the way from Warsaw for eight hours, we bought cash, we had a contract ready and we were keen to become an invisibobble partner."

Felix: "I appreciate that."

Shorter guy: "But you made us meet your INTERN."

Felix: "Intern? That was ME."

Shorter guy: "That was you? But that guy made us coffee! You were nowhere to be seen, so we left!"

Felix: "We're a start-up, we don't have interns. I negotiate prices, find the distributors, call retailers, email retailers, pitch to retailers, pitch to them again, talk to our manufacturer in China, do the quality control, clean invisibobbles if they're dirty, process orders, think about how we're going to grow, make sure bills are paid, write invoices, chase invoices, check invoices have been paid, order displays for hair shows, collect displays, drive to hair shows, put up the display, talk to potential customers, say the same thing over and over about how invisibobble doesn't dent your hair, learn about up-dos, talk to hairdressers, listen to customers – and I also make the coffee."

OK, he didn't give that entire list, but he did politely explain that, as we were a start-up, we did EVERYTHING ourselves. No interns, no coffee waiter, no staff.

A few weeks later, the tall and short Polish guys came back to Munich in their Mercedes, with their cool ten grand in cash. I went to the meeting with Felix this time, to confirm that the cash would indeed easily fit in a briefcase, and it was in crisp bundles of 25 €20 notes, so each bundle was €500, and there were 20 of those. It came in a sealed plastic bag, and as soon as the deal was done and the Polish guys were back on the road, we ripped it open. It was the most cash we'd ever seen, and we unbundled it and piled it all up on the table and threw it up in the air while taking videos on our phones and then replayed them in slow motion. After about an hour, we packed it all up and decided we should do the responsible thing and take it to the bank.

# 11.

# There Isn't a Box for That

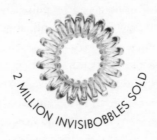

2 MILLION INVISIBOBBLES SOLD

**WHAT I LEARNED:**

- It's good to be the orange fish
- Hiring grown-ups can help your business
- Trade fairs are expensive but worth it

In autumn 2013, my third year of university, I moved into a two-bedroom flat. It had double-glazing and was in a modern block in central Leamington Spa, and the money we had made from invisibobble meant I could afford to live there alone. One or two people showed interest in renting the second bedroom, but I was perfectly happy doing my own thing.

I lived around the corner from The Benjamin Satchwell, a glass-fronted Wetherspoons pub on one of the town's main streets, where I'd spend a lot of time working. Satchwell was an 18<sup>th</sup> century shoemaker, postmaster and town mediator, and he discovered Leamington's second spring, which helped the village develop into a thriving town. He's known as the 'founding father' of Leamington Spa, so it was inspiring that I could work somewhere named after such a visionary.

I also wasn't really a library type of person; instead, my routine would be to get up, do some work on invisibobble, go to the university gym at around 11am, go for a coffee if I could afford it and work, go to the pub after lunch, manage invisibobble orders, stay in the pub until about 6pm and then go back to my flat.

Many of my friends were doing four-year courses, which included a year abroad in their third year, but mine was only three, meaning I had fewer mates around. My life was pretty different from the other students, who would go to the library on campus, about a 20-minute drive away, staying there from early morning until late at night. I would occasionally bump into people who would be surprised to see me, as they thought I was on a four-year course and would therefore be abroad. It never really bothered me that I was keeping to myself, because I felt I had my own life, and I was just so focused on invisibobble.

I remember Niki telling me once that he'd seen a poster at his school of a shoal of pale-coloured fish all swimming one way, and there was one orange fish going against the tide with a caption that said: "Be the orange fish." That image stayed with me, because anyone can go with what the masses are doing, or they can choose to be different. Being innovative or quirky is much more difficult, but at the same time, I think it's much more rewarding. I never really felt like I was missing out on anything.

When I did go to campus, a lot of the time I'd be writing invoices during lectures, as I've already said, or creating labels for DHL to dispatch goods, but no one really understood why I was prioritizing invisibobble. But I'd promised customers that

I'd be sending them hair ties that day, so I had to do the admin and that's just how it was.

During my final year, the big banks and management consultancies would come to the 'flattery fairs' on campus, where they would vie for students' attention by paying for drinks in a bar or giving away mugs. The idea would be that you turn up in a suit, shake hands, mingle with important people and try to impress them with your ambitions.

I would turn up, take a mug, drink the drinks, chat to my friends and then leave.

Founding a company while still at uni was a big thing in California but not in the British Midlands, and because invisibobble often got kind of an "Oh, it's just a hair tie, it doesn't count," type response from other students, I didn't say much about what I was doing, even when they specifically asked me about it.

I also had to go and see the university's careers counsellor during my third year. Like many unis, Warwick was very serious about students applying for a corporate role and having a job and a contract even before we'd finished our final year. One day, I got an email from the careers person in my department requesting a meeting God knows where on campus, so I trekked in, found the building and the room, which was numbered something like SWX19-A, and knocked on the door.

"Come in," a voice said.

I went in and sat down opposite a woman I'd never seen before and would probably never see again.

"Hi, Sophie," she said, looking down at a piece of paper with my name on it.

"How are things?" the woman asked.

"Fine."

"How are you feeling?"

"Fine."

"Are you happy?"

"Yes."

*Is this meant to be therapy?* I'm thinking. *Who is this woman anyway? Can I go now?*

"How are the job applications going? Can you tell me which consultancies and banks you've applied to?" she said, looking down at the form again.

"I'm not doing any."

The woman's face made a strange shape, one I doubted it had ever made before. She didn't say anything.

"I have my own hair tie business: invisibobble. We're sold on the high street."

"Invisi-what?" the woman said.

"invisibobble. It's going pretty well, and when I graduate, I am going to dedicate my full attention to it."

"There isn't a box for that," she said.

"OK, well I'm planning to move to Munich where our head office is after I graduate, and we are aiming to sell our products in 12 countries by the end of this year."

Her face returned to the strange shape, and she consulted the form again.

"Are you a people person?" she asked. "How about HR?"

Felix found the same thing: he had to do two placements as part of his course. The first one was at an investment bank and the second was at … invisibobble. He convinced his tutor to let him do a placement at his own business by saying he would otherwise quit his degree.

For me, I think a combination of admiring Red Bull for its unconventional approach to business, with maybe a bit of the risk-taking nature of my dad, and a love for fashion that I've always had, all pushed me toward doing my own thing. It's a shame that entrepreneurship wasn't part of the university's aspirations for students at the time, although now I think the university has a much stronger focus on entrepreneurs.

In 2013, our second year of trading, invisibobble made $1.1 million (about £860,000) in revenue and we were able to start paying ourselves a modest salary. It felt like the right time to do this because we had made a decent amount of money after reinvesting most of our profit back into the business.

Growing a lot in 2013 was great, and it meant we had contracts with several distributors and wholesalers going into 2014. Wholesalers carry a variety of products that they either buy directly from a manufacturer or from distributors, and they usually supply a variety of different products to several different outlets.

Felix and I decided to invest in a stand at Cosmoprof in Bologna in spring 2014, probably the largest hair and beauty trade show in the world. It's a four-day event, which now has more than 3,000 exhibitors and around 250,000 visitors in about 15 halls. Everyone – from people who make chairs for hair salons to injection moulding companies that produce packaging for face creams – goes to Cosmoprof, and they sit alongside huge companies like L'Oréal that might spend millions on a stand showing off their latest products.

We spent about $22,000 (about £17,000) on a stand for invisibobble, which was a MASSIVE investment for us, and the first time we had spent big on marketing.

It was also the first time we felt ignored by the industry.

Exhibiting at a trade show is a huge amount of work. They give you the basic booth, but the rest is up to you. Even though invisibobbles are tiny products, we had boxes and boxes of them, plus massive posters of our hair ties in people's hair, a big poster with our logo and product pictures. We also had flyers with details of invisibobble and our contact information, and we had a hairdresser with us who would do up-dos with invisibobbles. She would get people on to the stand by telling them it would only take two minutes to do their hair, and then time how long it took to do it. The up-dos were great because then people had invisibobbles in their hair and would talk to their friends or colleagues about them, and maybe wear one around their wrist. It was a talking point.

Exhibitors got access to the show an hour or so before it opened at 9.30am to set up, and about ten minutes before it opened a voice came over the tannoy:

"Welcome to Cosmoprof. You have T-minus ten minutes until the show opens. Hope – it is the only thing stronger than fear. May the odds be ever in your favour."

OK, the last bit is from *The Hunger Games* but, to me, that's how the announcement sounded, and each day it made me feel like, "Yes! The game is ON!"

All day, until 6.30pm, we were 'on,' every day, for four days. As we were expanding, we had hired a head of international sales, Zelda, who also came with us to the show.

Only, no one wanted to talk to us.

People would walk past our booth, and Felix and I would stand there, smiling. Sometimes they would show a bit of interest and one of us would say, "Hi, are you familiar with invisibobble?" Mostly, the answer was no. I'd start speaking, and then I'd notice the person looking over my shoulder at Zelda, who was maybe around 50 years old. I'd say, "I'm the founder, do you have any questions?" and the person would say, "Oh, I'll wait to speak to her," motioning toward Zelda.

At Cosmoprof, young women (and men, though back then it was mostly women) would hand out flyers for products, suppliers or talks happening in different areas of the show. At this point I was 21 (and looked younger), and people thought I was just a flyer girl, or maybe the hair model, which is why they would want to speak with Zelda, who looked more like a proper grown-up. Sometimes they would finish their takeaway coffee while we were speaking and then they'd hand me the empty cup to dispose of.

Then, they would walk over to Zelda, and she would talk to them and I could tell by their body language that she was finding out whether they were a distributor or a wholesaler or whatever, and Felix and I would go and do something else on the stand. We couldn't hear Zelda's conversations, but after a while, there would be a gesture toward us, and she'd be explaining that Felix and I had founded invisibobble two years before. Then I'd see an expression of "oh" on the woman's or man's face, or "I don't believe it," because we looked (and were) so young. Then we would tell the story of invisibobble, trying to explain it like it was the first time we'd ever said it, telling people that it's hair-loving (which is what hair professionals are particularly interested in) and so on. This happened maybe 50 times a day, every day, for four days.

You can't leave products or anything on your stand because people might steal them. At a show we did in Dubai a year or so later, we had a woman grab a whole bunch of invisibobble packs, and we had to chase after her. At the end of each day, we'd pack everything up, which took ages. Because the show halls are so massive, we'd walk for miles with boxes and boxes, backing up through various sets of double doors, dropping a box (which would inevitably land the wrong way up, spilling invisibobbles all over the floor) picking it up and carrying on.

And because it's so intense, the tendency is to roll to a bar after each long day, forget to eat, get accidentally, totally drunk, wake up the next day with a huge headache, thinking, "How did that happen?" and then do exactly the same after the show that night. This is why, even now, trade shows are the most exhausting things we ever do.

When the response to invisibobble was negative, we learned not to get offended. It's not a product for everyone but, for me, it's important that our spiral hair ties are for the vast majority of people. To start with, it's kind of a slap in the face when people say things that are less than positive, but you have to let it go. We also found we'd need to hire some Italian staff for the next show, because very often people would speak Italian to us and I'd have to answer in a mixture of Spanish (which I'd learned from my mum, growing up) and English, and we'd somehow get by.

In the end, the reaction was overwhelmingly positive, but it took a while for us to sign any business from the show.

Cosmoprof ended up being the last commitment I made to invisibobble during university, because after that I had to write all my essays and prepare for my final exams.

# 12.

# Mei and the Missing invisibobble Factory, Part One

**WHAT I LEARNED:**

- If you don't focus on operations, it can kill your business
- Get weather insurance if you have a factory overseas or anywhere
- Don't let your cofounder go to the other side of the world

Felix's university course was four years long and included a semester abroad. Where did he choose to go?

Sydney, Australia.

I'm not joking.

He went to the other side of the world, just as invisibobble was really taking off in the summer of 2014. To be fair, he was working really hard on invisibobble, but it's just not the same being in a completely different time zone. I totally supported his decision to go there, even though it meant things were a bit tougher for me.

I had done my final university exams in June, and in July found out that I'd got a 2.1, which I was happy with, given how much time invisibobble was taking up. (The British degree system is ranked as follows: first, or 1, which is for exceptional students; 2.1, which is for pretty darn good ones; 2.2 is OK; and third, or 3, means you were mostly in the pub or club, but you scraped by.)

As soon as I finished my exams, I moved to Munich and spent most of the time in the office above the nightclub because we had orders constantly coming in.

This was a critical time for invisibobble and is the period when some start-ups fail, because they *have* to focus on getting the operations of the business right, and that means ordering enough products from the manufacturer to be delivered in the right amount to the right customer at the right time. If customers don't get what they ordered, they have to explain that to the salon or store, and it can mean empty shelves, which is bad for the store and bad for invisibobble.

Cash flow can get disrupted. If orders don't arrive with customers, you won't get paid until they do and, even then, payment terms can be as long as 120 days, which is a long time to wait for money in any business.

It's very common for new (and established) businesses to borrow money from the bank or raise funds from investors, but it's never something we wanted to do, or have done, with invisibobble. So that meant we had to keep a strict eye on our cash flow, and if there were any delays in supplying products to anyone, we had to sort it out immediately. We are in business for the long term and, for us, taking outside investment would mean being answerable to someone else. The nature of invisibobble is that our start-up costs were low, and we were profitable from the start. While I'm ambitious for the business, I'm all about long-term brand building rather than a quick sale. And that brand building means reinvesting money, and investing love, into the product and business.

By summer 2014, the phone had started to ring every five minutes, with some distributor or other complaining that an order hadn't arrived or had taken a little bit longer than usual, and where was it? For every call or email I got, I had to go onto the DHL website, type in the tracking number, find out where our parcel was, and then call the distributor back. We had no business systems in place, no automated tracking or invoicing, no IT. We were doing everything via Excel, Word and emails. The shit would hit the fan almost every day.

As I mentioned, we had hired a head of sales, Zelda, and I started to hand over my and Felix's customers over to her. But, especially as we were founders, those customers would really flip when we tried to explain that Zelda would be handling their business from now on. If those customers owned their companies, they liked to do business with other owners, or founders. But we couldn't do that for the rest of our lives or invisibobble would stagnate and we'd never get past dealing with distributors.

We would hand over a client to Zelda, and sometimes they'd hate it, feeling that they were more important than that. They'd call Felix, and he'd say, "I'm in Australia, call Zelda," or they'd call me just as I was in the middle of handing their account over to Zelda.

Suddenly, amid all of this, to my horror, I discovered we were receiving a lot less product from China than we'd ordered. By this time, invisibobbles would come ready packaged in their packs of three, but we were only getting about a fifth of what we had ordered.

But wait a minute, I need to introduce another character into the story: Mei Huang. Mei is a woman who Felix met at a trade show, and she acted as our agent. She's a Chinese woman based in Germany and speaks fluent German, and she helped us source a manufacturer in China when we were ready to move on from Liang, our supplier from Alibaba.

We totally relied on Mei for everything, from finding our new production facility to translating emails, agreeing on prices with the factory, answering questions if deliveries got held up and so on. It was very important for us that all of our invisibobbles were made in one place, because our production facilities needed to be of a certain standard and ready to be audited. Retailers have strict safety requirements and standards for workers, and we needed to be sure we could meet those criteria.

As a result of still not receiving our orders, I called Mei.

"Hi," I said, trying to retain a positive tone.

"Sophie! Hi. How are you?" Mei said.

"Fine, but we're having some problems with orders not arriving."

"Problem? Sure. Let me look into it."

A few days passed, and then a week. Meanwhile, we were taking orders from our customers and passing them on to China, via Mei, and all of them were being accepted. I had emailed Mei and she'd assured me that our orders would arrive 'soon,' or that they were 'on their way.' But then a week went by and then another. Still no major deliveries.

Finally, after three weeks, I got the truth out of Mei.

There had been a typhoon in China, and our production site had been underwater for three weeks. Three weeks! I could not believe it.

In Chinese business, there's a culture of saving face, or not wanting to disappoint, and so instead of telling us immediately there had been a problem, Mei had put it off. Which actually made things worse.

And so I had to send out a kind of alarm email to all of our distributors, saying we were having 'capacity problems' and we would need to ration their orders and that, proportionately, they would be getting maybe a fifth of what they ordered.

At the same time, we started getting the largest single orders we had ever received, like, "Hi, can I order 20,000 units please?" "Hi, can I order 50,000 units please?" "Hi, I would like to take all the stock in your warehouse, when can you deliver by?" The demand was off the charts.

And I knew there was no stock in our warehouse. That just made our customers want more: as soon as I told them there was a limited supply, they would compete with each other to get the most stock possible. (Later, we tried that as a kind of reverse psychology strategy: we told customers there was limited stock and then waited for the orders to roll in. It didn't work.)

We had to ration orders for about four months, and it took us about six months to properly catch up with all of them. I'd get to the office for eight in the morning and there was no chance I was leaving before ten at night, just to try to manage the emails and the orders. Our production facility had to be reconstructed from scratch.

---

In spite of the typhoon, 2014 was a massive year for invisibobble.

In Germany, we had got the listing in the posh perfumery, but we still needed to go mass market. A large, mass-market drug store chain was interested but, like some other retailers, they wanted us to make an own-label version for them. As I've said, this is pretty common with retailers, who would often say they didn't sell branded hair accessories, only their own label.

If there's no proof that the idea works, they want to take the less risky route and brand it under their own label.

We also found out the hard way that if a branded product sells more than it's expected to, retailers will very quickly make their own versions. Some manufacturers' sales teams, under pressure to sell products to retailers, sometimes agree to make an own-label version, but I have always insisted that invisibobble won't do that.

But the fact that we were getting better known via press coverage and blogs in Germany helped us. This still surprises me, but men as well as women would ask what that spiral thing was on their friend's wrist and it was a topic of conversation. And because you couldn't get our hair ties everywhere – known as selective distribution – we were kind of the beauty industry's best-kept secret.

When we finally persuaded the mass-market German pharmacy chain to stock three-packs of clear invisibobbles, which they did in November 2014, it became one of its most successful hair category launches ever. When you finally make a desired product available to the masses, people jump at it. What's so crazy as well was that when most brands do a new launch like that, they would spend hundreds of thousands or more on marketing, and we spent nothing. Our budget was zero. Part of the reason we got into that retailer was the cardboard stands we also provided for free (which was the only thing we spent marketing money on), and this helped us get around the problem of stores telling us they had no room.

We started the year in 13 European countries, and by the end of the year we were in 30 countries. Our turnover 15-folded from the start to the end of the year and we were delighted. Without the typhoon, I think we could have 30-folded our business. In 2014 alone, we made £5.2 million (about $6.7 million) in revenue – and I had only graduated during the summer of that year.

# 13.

# Is Imitation the Highest Form of Flattery?

13 MILLION INVISIBOBBLES SOLD

**WHAT I LEARNED:**

- **Business can be brutal**
- **Fakes are fucking awful**
- **Focusing on making the brand the best it can be will help to fight copies**

You know when you're a kid and you go to the bowling alley, and they put those bumpers on the sides of the lanes to stop the ball rolling off so you can have a better shot at the skittles? Well, we were naive enough to think that this would be the case for us kids with our own company, that somehow the big business world would put guardrails up for us, because we were young and new to it. We had a lot of encouragement from the people who knew us, especially me, being a 'female entrepreneur,' and looking back I probably had a little bit of a protective bubble around me, being from an underrepresented group.

But in 2014, the year of the typhoon, those guardrails definitely came off. How?

One word: fakes.

The first time I knew we'd been copied was when I was sitting in the office at my aeroplane wing desk, scrolling through invisibobble's Facebook page. I was alone in the office, Felix was in Australia, and the New Flag team was out. I came across a comment by one of our up-do videos, which went something like this:

"The first time I bought invisibobbles they were great, but I've bought another packet and they're really shit. I put one in my hair just now to do a ponytail and it snapped. DO NOT BUY THIS PRODUCT!!!!! Also, the packet wasn't quite the same as usual."

My blood ran cold. I responded immediately with my email address, writing: "Hi, thanks for this and I'm sorry you've had this problem. Could you send me a picture of the hair tie and the packaging?"

A few minutes later, the email came through. The woman said she had bought them from a Russian hair salon, and the picture of the packaging looked exactly like ours. But just looking at the image, I could tell that the cube was maybe half a centimetre shorter than real invisibobble packaging, but it still had our name, our logo, and our lines on it, like "the traceless hair ring," and "hair loving." *Everything* looked identical, apart from the size.

*Fuck.*

I can't explain how angry I was at this, but I was so completely furious that someone could create fake everything and pretend they were real invisibobbles. It meant that someone, somewhere, had briefed a factory (in China) to take our hair ties and cute boxes and copy them, and that distributors, salons and consumers would think they were real, and then blame us when they snapped, or got stuck in their hair. They were nothing but cheap rip-offs.

The *one* good thing about a direct fake, where someone has copied your product, word for word, is that you know you can contact all of the distributors and wholesalers to ask them to check whether their products are real or not. As we later learned, when you see fakes that look more or less the same, but have just changed the brand name a bit, you don't know how they have got onto the market, or who is selling them, and it's much harder to trace where the problem came from.

I started calling and emailing all of our distributors and retailers. I guess I was expecting some sympathy, but what I actually got from some of the people was anger. People blamed invisibobble for letting the fakes onto the market, and they were very upset because they had spent money on them, and I had to ask them to destroy them and then send a proof of destruction certificate. We got some hatred, and they would try to pass the costs on to us (we refused) but, in the long run, it helped to stop the fakes from circulating and eventually made all of our partners check whether they were getting authorized goods.

We also asked customs in European countries to put import seizures on things labelled 'invisibobble,' which meant they would check what was inside boxes that arrived at the border. We managed to stop some fakes this way, but it was only a very small portion of the copies that got in. We also tried to put export seizures on goods going out of China. You pay a fee every year to do this, but we've never had anything seized, because often fake goods coming out of China get labelled as something else entirely.

The delay in production caused by the typhoon also meant that other copies had a chance to come on to the market. There was a clear demand for our product but, once it became unavailable, other distributors (who we didn't work with) saw the opportunity to make their own versions. One of these was called EZbobbles, which copied our cube packaging, circular logo and used our tagline, too. Posts on Instagram said things like, "The design will not harm the hair," but also referred to us, "a good alternative to invisibobble." At least they knew who they were copying and kind of acknowledged that we were the original (and the best!). But I could tell just by looking at pictures of EZbobbles that the two ends of the coil that makes our hair ties circular had been soldered together poorly, as I could see an ugly lump. EZbobbles also copied the little cardboard pyramid displays we have in hairdressers. *Again, fuck.*

The problem when copies like this come onto the market is that consumers don't necessarily know the difference between them and us, especially early on when we were not an established brand. People were also not used to hair ties being branded at all, because they were used to shops' own brand of hair elastics, which would usually mean multiple hair ties stapled to a cardboard backing.

But because copies like this used the exact product claims, word for word, that we had on our packaging and had copyrighted, we had grounds for a legal case against the salons and retailers that sold them.

At one point, trying to manage the tide of fakes was my full-time job. I'd work out who the distributors of the copies were by the salons they were sold in and I'd call them up, mainly sitting at my desk, alone, in the tiny Munich office. I'd sit up straight in my chair, cross my legs, cough and put my best stern voice on.

"Hi. I'm from invisbobble's legal department," I'd say, trying to maintain my composure. "I noticed you are selling EZbobble, which has copied us. Because EZbobble has copied our copyrighted product claims, we are mounting a legal case against them, and we need you to stop selling them straightaway." I'd use as much legal language as I could, keeping my voice persuasive and strict.

Sometimes the response would be positive. Other times I would have to push harder, still sitting alone in the office, aged 21 and trying to sound older and wiser. "I'm holding our lawyers off at the moment because we would much rather resolve this without their involvement, but if the products are still being sold in a week I will have to issue a cease and desist letter," and then I'd send a follow-up email with my signature as Head of Intellectual Property and Compliance, instead of Managing Partner. A cease and desist letter is a legal document you send to stop illegal activity, and you can threaten to sue someone if they keep selling the product.

One thing we thought we couldn't do much about legally were the copies of the product itself. We had been told by numerous lawyers that we couldn't patent the shape of invisibobble, because the coiled shape is commonly known in things like telephone cords already. But that would eventually come back to bite us.

At one point we had a massive problem with copies in the UK, partly because of how we set up our distribution. We had signed agreements with several companies that meant they would be the exclusive distributor for a particular region. That was a mistake, because it meant that the hair salons the distributors didn't cover couldn't get invisibobble. Then other distributors in the same region would get angry.

As invisibobble is pretty easy for a distributor to sell to a hairdresser because it's so small and light, other distributors would want to be able to sell it too. They had been hearing about the success of invisibobble, but as we had signed exclusive agreements in some areas (which, in hindsight, was a mistake, but we knew nothing to start with), some of the distributors that couldn't get invisibobble started making their own copies that seemed to flood UK hair salons at one point.

They looked pretty similar, but the quality was not as good. We were very particular when we were developing our packaging to ensure it didn't scratch easily or become static as we didn't want packs to attract dust on the shelves or in someone's home. That wasn't noticeable to the naked eye, though, and it really made it look like anyone could copy us.

Another time, one of our largest UK wholesalers called us one day and said they would no longer be carrying invisibobble, and they just stopped ordering. This was a pretty big deal for us, because they were ordering about $330,000 (around £250,000) of products a year from us. The wholesaler said something like they wanted to "go down a different path." There was something in the guy's tone of voice that made me realize *they were doing a copy*. So, for a couple of weeks we would stalk them on the internet, checking their website and Twitter to see what they were doing. One day there it was, their version of invisibobble, displayed online with all the other products they sold, and using some of our copyrighted material. At least that meant we could sue them, and they had to tell us who all of their customers were, so we could make sure they could get real invisibobbles.

It even got to the point that we would be exhibiting at a hairdressing trade show and we'd see copies of our brand on another stand. Once, at a show called Salon International, which is held in London every year, we had a beautiful stand, with lovely displays and a hairdresser doing up-dos and we saw a copy I'm going to call Bububobble on display at another stand.

At the show, a middle-aged balding man with a paunch appeared. He looked rather like a slug: a slug that hadn't seen sun, or daylight for that matter, in the last decade.

He slugged his way over to our stand and said, "Hi, I want to talk to the boss."

"Hello, I'm one of the founders, how can I help?" I replied. He looked me up and down as if to say, *but you're a child.*

"Well, I'm from Bububobble. We're selling our hair ties £2 cheaper than yours, but I guess you knew that," he said, with a smug expression. "How're things going for ya?" he asked, waiting to see how I felt about him selling his crappy hair ties for less than ours.

"Yes, we've been in touch via our lawyers, I think. Things are going really well, thanks. We've just launched our new collection and we've been sold in Boots now for a while, as well as Urban Outfitters, and we're having fun too," I said.

"Well, you're not going to have fun for long, are ya?" the old guy said and went back to his stand.

I didn't care too much for the Bububobble guy. In a weird way, it was almost disappointing that we got copied by the kind of old sods who probably have 1,000 regrets about their lives and have nothing better to do than copy some teenagers who created a new hair tie, and then try to create some excitement for themselves by coming over to us at a trade fair to demean our products and make themselves feel superior. If Mr Bububobble had done something creative and inspiring in hair accessories, I might have had some respect for him. The people who copied us were often similar to Mr Bububobble: ageing guys who didn't really make an effort with anything, from their bodies to their business, who were just lazily hoping to make a quick buck.

I think the people who ripped us off did it because they thought it would be an easy way to make a quick buck, that our hair ties and cube packaging would be simple to copy, and they could just ask their Chinese factories to replicate us. But it is actually pretty complicated to make something as simple as an invisibobble well, making sure the colours are consistent and the quality is good, and coming up with fun and creative names for new colours and styles.

We also have an advantage – because the copycats think it's so easy, their copies end up looking cheap and inferior. They also have a hard time getting into mainstream retailers, because the quality is always poor and because they are obvious copies.

The Bububobble conversation at the trade fair wasn't the only time we came face-to-face with the rip-off merchants.

I'm going to jump forward a bit to spring 2015, when we went to Cosmoprof in Bologna for the second time. Again, we had spent about $22,000 (around £17,000) on a stand there and, as usual, would get accidentally totally drunk most nights and spend the days running on adrenaline, coffee and Red Bull.

Parts of the show are divided into different countries, so that people can find beauty products from their own region. About 150 feet from our stand at the show, there was a tent called the Chinese Pavilion.

The year before, I'd seen fake Tangle Teezers in the Chinese section, so I was a bit anxious about what I might find this time. On a rare break, I decided to check it out with Felix. We walked around, noticing hair straighteners, salon chairs, shampoos and hairbrushes at booths of all different shapes and sizes, many of them with a backdrop of a blown-up photograph of a Western woman looking dreamily into the camera while her perfect shiny hair blew sideways, often using the same picture to sell different products.

Then suddenly, I saw it. My heart skipped a beat. I started sweating and feeling panicky.

There was a whole, entire, fake invisibobble stand, which was EXACTLY the same as ours.

Just as with the Russian copy the woman wrote about on Facebook, the packaging was the same, the logo was identical, only we were seeing it all replicated in real life, at a booth that anyone from anywhere could walk by. They even used the same photographs as us! We had used Niki's girlfriend Talia at the time to be our hair model, and there she was, larger than life, a massive image of her covering the back wall of their booth; the exact same image we had at our stand, 150 feet away, at the same trade fair. Hell, they had also gone so far as to use the name New Flag.

I couldn't stop myself. I ran up to the guy at the stand.

"You are copying our products! You need to REMOVE THIS IMMEDIATELY. ALL OF IT!"

The guy, a Chinese man in his early 30s, just looked at me and raised his eyebrows.

"Qual è il problema?" he asked, in Italian.

"Il problema? IL PROBLEMA?!"

I don't speak Italian, so I shouted, in Spanish: "¡Estás copiando nuestros productos! Tienes que quitar esto inmediatamente. TODO."

("You are copying our products! You need to REMOVE THIS IMMEDIATELY. ALL OF IT!")

He understood some of that but shook his head.

"Non rimuovo nulla. Questo è il mio marchio, queste sono le mie fotografie."

That's when I lost it.

"NON RIMUOVO NULLA? NON RIMUOVO NULLA!" (I guessed that meant "I won't remove anything.")

"THAT IS **TALIA** ON THE WALL," I shouted in English. "TALIA!!! SHE IS OUR MODEL. THESE ARE NOT YOUR PHOTOGRAPHS. **THESE ARE NOT YOUR PHOTOGRAPHS!**"

I started picking his fake invisibobbles up and putting them on the floor. I grabbed handfuls of his flyers, which also had our pictures on them. I tugged at the poster of Talia. While I was doing that, he picked up all of the boxes of hair ties and put them back on the stand. Then I tried to open the suitcase he had at the back of the booth, but it was locked. I pushed the fake invisibobbles onto the floor again, and the guy was so close that when he shouted at me to stop in Italian, I got bubbles of his spit on my face.

I turned to Felix.

"What are we going to do?"

"Tell him we're going to the police," Felix said.

"Vamos a la policia!" I shouted, in Spanish (I figured the Italian and Spanish for "police" must be similar.) Then I remembered the word "Carabinieri," the name of the Italian police.

"CARABINIERI! CARABINIERI!" I screamed.

He finally reacted to this and moved to start taking down the packs of fake invisibobbles.

"OK. I'm watching you!" I said, pointing two fingers at my eyes and back at him.

I couldn't believe that Cosmoprof would allow copies in, especially when we were only 150 feet apart.

We went back to our stand, and I was feeling kind of good about myself. I had cracked one of the fake manufacturers!

A couple hours later, I went back to the stand.

It was all back up, in exactly the same way as it had been before. The guy was busy with a customer, who was putting a fake invisibobble into her hair. I tried to remain calm and went back to our booth.

Felix and I went to Cosmoprof's intellectual property office and showed them pictures of the fake booth. They were sympathetic but explained that they couldn't do anything about it without proof that the copyright for the photographs belonged to us and asked us to get the relevant documents.

So I called Niki and explained the situation.

"We don't have those documents," came the voice down the phone.

"What do you mean, you DON'T HAVE THE DOCUMENTS? There is a man at Cosmoprof and he's using huge pictures of your girlfriend only feet away from our invisibobble stand AND YOU DON'T HAVE THE DOCUMENTS TO PROVE THEY ARE OUR PHOTOS??!!"

Turns out, we actually didn't have the rights to the photos, which is a classic mistake for a start-up to make. We had no clue that we even needed to negotiate any kind of rights, and of course we found out at the worst moment possible when we had only hours to sort something out. Luckily, Niki knew the photographer pretty well and asked him to transfer the rights to us. They wrote a contract, got it signed and scanned it to us at Cosmoprof.

The head office guy came with us to the Chinese-Italian guy's stand, with the paperwork, and instructed him to take the photos down. It didn't seem to be a simple process, because there was a lot of talk, and gesturing toward the pictures and the Chinese-Italian was going up to the photos and pushing them and then turning back to the head office guy and waving his hands around.

The head office guy turned to me and said, "He will take the products down but is it OK if he leaves the photographs?"

I couldn't quite believe what I was hearing, but now I knew why there had been so much arm waving. The photographs were attached to the frames of the booth and were part of the walls, so taking the photos down effectively meant destroying the booth. *Excellent*, I said to myself in a *Simpsons* Mr Burns voice, touching my hands together by their finger pads. *Excellent*.

"I don't care. If you need to get a knife and rip it out of the wall, I don't care."

And that's what the Chinese-Italian guy did. He slashed and tore and ripped the photographs. He was pretty angry, and then he got up on a chair and started throwing everything else from his shelves onto the floor.

"Are you happy now?" he said, in Italian, the head office guy translated.

"I don't care that you have taken the time to fake our hair ties, copy our packaging and flown all the way from China with all your suitcases. I don't care that this stand has probably cost you $30,000. I really don't care," I said.

I'll never know whether the head office guy translated what I said.

After all of our experiences with fakes and copies (and there have been several more), what I realized was, the more we focused on the brand, on making it the best it can be, getting the small details right, being creative with names and the designs on our cute three-packs, and a relentless focus on quality, the more the fakers would find it hard to take customers away from us, and some of the copycats (including Bububobble) have just gone away as a result.

That's not to say they aren't a threat. At one point in 2014 I really thought we were finished because of all the copies. I had echoes in my head of people telling me that spiral hair ties would just be a short-term fashion trend, a fad that would eventually disappear, and I thought that the copies could be the beginning of the end, and that I might have to apply to management consulting after all.

But what I kept saying to the doubters was, "I don't think so, because the product has a functional benefit that is fundamentally different to the elastic hair ties that already exist, and if we make sure ours are the best quality, with the biggest distribution, then we have a great future." And I told myself that you can copy soap and toothpaste and whatnot, and yet, huge companies that make branded soap and toothpaste still do just fine.

At the end of the day, there will always be the customer who prefers the original invisibobble and the customer who prefers a cheap copy. What is important is that they understand the difference between the two, and I'm talking about "me too" products, those that are very similar to ours but aren't direct fakes. I sometimes see comments on social media like: "I got my invisibobble copies today," and I think, *OK fine, they've made the active decision to go for the cheaper version*. I mean how much can you expect a 13-year-old girl to spend on her hair? There are shops that service the younger end of the market and they play a role, but our core consumer is actually a woman in her 20s who buys invisibobbles for herself, and we also find that older women will buy them for themselves and their younger daughters.

We now focus on being the best and the biggest and at the forefront of innovation. Our responsibility, as the brand that invented this new product, is to be what they call 'category king': to be the leader that creates more, fun and different hair ties that people love, because they have never seen anything like it before.

(Top)
After giving my TEDx speech about invisibobble in Copenhagen in November 2015.

(Left)
In my Christmas holidays in Verbier 2019 where I finished my manuscript for this book.

*(Top)*
One of two trucks ready to leave our production site in China in 2019 with the single largest order we had ever received for one single product type. It amounted to 11.1 million hair ties.

*(Right)*
A delivery truck that burned down during transport with our invisibobbles inside. Thankfully no one was hurt in the accident.

*(Top)* Our wavers (hair clips) being produced in Germany, 2019.

*(Middle)* An example of how our wavers were breaking shortly after launch — this was a big disaster for us. We thankfully reacted quickly and got it fixed for the next production run.

*(Bottom)* The bathroom in one of the factories we visited in China which manufactures spiral shaped hair ties for other companies that distribute them worldwide.

*(Top)*
Felix and me at the office in 2014, after landing a big distribution deal. We were in a good mood!

*(Bottom)*
Me in a pub in Warwick in 2012, shortly after founding invisibobble.

*(Top right)*
Felix and me exhibiting at our first big tradeshow in 2014, Cosmoprof Bologna.

*(Bottom right)*
Daniel and Niki, the co-founder on New Flag, at Octoberfest in Munich, 2019.

*(Top)*
Me at a tradeshow in Dubai.

*(Bottom)*
Me visiting the 'invisibobble wall' at a big retail chain store in Los Angeles.

*(Top right)*
Our invisibobble Christmas collection 2019.

*(Bottom right)*
One of our 'Cheat Day' collection items. The hair ties themselves were scented like sweet treats.

Our invisibobble
ORIGINAL –
the first product
we launched,
and the most
famous product
in our portfolio.

# 14.
# All the Worms in China

15 MILLION INVISIBOBBLES SOLD

**WHAT I LEARNED:**

- **Chinese culture can be a huge shock**
- **Cleanliness standards can be different in China**
- **You have to work hard to get answers**

After the production facility got destroyed by a typhoon and we weren't told about it for weeks, we decided we needed to go to China to understand more about how our hair ties were made and look for backup factories in case this, or something similar, ever happened again. We were also having minor quality control issues by that time, and because we'd started operating at a reasonably large scale, those issues were becoming a bigger deal. We noticed colour variations between batches – sometimes Submarine Yellow looked more like High-Vis Jacket Yellow, which wasn't a colour we wanted, and sometimes we noticed our invisibobbles were thicker than usual

– and you can't have those kinds of variations when you are supplying retailers.

We were asking Mei why there were inconsistencies, and we didn't feel we were always getting straight answers from the production facility. We wanted to know how the factory was organized, how many invisibobbles they made every day, how they made sure there were no bottlenecks in production, and to check that workers had enough breaks and were treated fairly.

We first visited in June 2015, when Felix had finished his degree (he got a first, of course). Our production facility was near the port city of Qingdao (known for Tsingtao beer) on the east coast, which is about a 15-hour flight from Germany, with a transfer in Beijing.

At the time, there was a system in China where foreigners had to stay in at least a four-star hotel, which you'd think would mean there'd be a certain standard and basic things like checking in would not be a problem. But because my mother is Spanish and my father is Danish, I have two passports, and a Danish as well as a Spanish spelling of my name (I use the Danish version). I've since learned from travelling 120 days a year that booking everything in my Danish name and then using only my Danish passport is the best idea, because anything else often confuses immigration officers.

But anyway, after a long flight from Munich to Qingdao, Felix and I finally arrived at our hotel, which was a well-known five-star chain. Getting out of our taxi, we went into a grand entrance with a high ceiling and lots of red and gold. As we approached the reception desk, we were met with a blank face. I'm thinking, *I'm standing here, suitcase in hand, giving you my passport, what do you think I'm trying to do?* I think maybe their booking system had everything in Chinese characters, which made it very hard for them to know what to do, but it took about

45 minutes for the receptionist to find a kitchen staff member who spoke English who could translate.

We got to our room, starving and exhausted, and decided to order room service dinner. The menu was in English as well as Chinese, so we could see things like spaghetti Bolognese, fish and chips, that kind of thing. We managed to order, in English, two standard club sandwiches, with chicken, bacon, salad and so on.

Eventually, our sandwiches arrived. Felix took a bite, froze, took the sandwich out of his mouth and put it on the plate. There was a WORM frantically crawling out of the sandwich, moving caterpillar-like toward the rim of the plate, totally confused by its new environment.

Felix called reception.

"Hi. There is a worm in our food."

"What?" came the answer. "No worm in food. Is bread, and chicken and bacon!"

"No, I know what's IN a club sandwich. As well as three pieces of toast and all the other things in a normal club sandwich, there is ALSO a worm," Felix said.

The woman came up to our room. The worm was still on the plate, building up the courage to escape somehow, and the woman kind of shrugged.

"We would like another club sandwich. With no worm," Felix said.

"No worm?" she asked.

"NO WORM," Felix said.

"What would you like in the sandwich?" the woman said.

"Bread, lettuce, chicken, bacon and tomato. And no worm. Like on the menu."

Desperately trying to stay awake through our hunger, we waited an hour and then finally, there was a knock at the door.

A small, white, tower of toast appeared on the plate, with small, green pieces of lettuce sticking out of the sides. We peeled back one of the slices of bread.

The club sandwich turned out to be just bread, then a layer of lettuce, another piece of bread, some more lettuce, and a final slice of bread.

I don't even think there was any butter or mayo on it. We gave up and went to bed.

———

It was a three-hour drive from Qingdao to our production facility and we wanted to get there early, around 8am, to make sure we could spend as much of the day there as possible. So, the next day, we got up at 4.30am and Mei picked us up with a driver at 5am, and drove out of town, the roads quickly turning from sealed to unpaved tracks.

After bumping along these tracks for several hours, we arrived at a small, rickety-looking building on the outskirts of a village, which Mei announced was our production facility. *This is our production facility* I thought and looked at Felix with raised eyebrows and probably an exhausted, pale, jetlagged face.

We went inside, into quite a long, dark, narrow room, with a window at one end and a heavy-looking machine with a metal funnel and a long conveyor belt with metal sides. This was the extrusion machine, which turned coloured plastic pellets into straight, long pieces, a bit like lengths of spaghetti. These long bits of material would be spat out of the machine, and there was a pile of them on the floor at one end. Then they would be wrapped around a hot bar of metal to make them into a spiral shape, before being cut into pieces, and then each end would be soldered together to finish the invisibobble hair ring.

Before we could start asking any questions, we had to meet the production manager and have tea, and we sat down in a small room just next to where the machine was. The furniture was exactly how you might imagine it: grand, high-backed Chinese chairs with gilt around the edge and furry cushions. Next to the chairs was a desk with a computer with a big, three-dimensional screen, which must have been from the 1980s. All the surfaces I could see had a thin layer of dust all over them.

Next to the computer was another low table, with an electric cooker and a saucepan full of water standing on it, and a metal tray at the bottom with a grill on top that collected any water that overflowed. All this was sitting on a soaking wet, tea-stained cloth. We sat down on the ornate chairs and the factory manager Xin brought out tiny, chipped cups, some of which had staples covering the cracks. Xin was in charge of producing our invisibobbles and Mei managed him, updating us on the process as we went along. This was the first time we'd met Xin.

The tea was part of the traditional Chinese hospitality, and the worst thing you can do is not drink it.

"There's no chance in hell I'm drinking that," Felix said, at that point. Felix has a thing about bacteria.

"OK, I'll take one for the team this time," I said, nodding and smiling and knowing that Xin wouldn't understand us.

I took a sip, thinking *I may or may not die after this*, and then smiled again at Xin. But he immediately topped my tiny cup up as well as Felix's, even though Felix hadn't drunk any. I put my cup down on the grill after taking another sip, and he refilled it, so it overflowed on to the cloth, and dripped down onto the floor, soaking the mat. He kept refilling it even though I hadn't drunk any more, and the tea trickled down again.

All the time this was going on, we tried to ask questions of Xin, via Mei, about how he organized the factory, how he found people to work there and why the unsealed invisibobbles were in a pile on the floor.

"How often do you clean the machine?" I asked. Mei translated. There was silence for a while.

Then Mei turned to us: "Clean?"

"Yes. You know, the machine is dirty, it looks like it hasn't been cleaned in a while."

Then there was a five-minute conversation between Mei and Xin and eventually Mei said: "He doesn't clean the machine."

This made me feel slightly sick: if this is how he treats his machines, how does he treat the tea he serves? And how can our invisibobbles be clean if they run through this machine?

At some point, I needed the toilet, so I asked to be shown where it was. It was through another room and left at the end, Mei said, pointing to a door a few feet from the soaking tea table.

I opened the door, to what turned out to be a bedroom. It was FULL of stuff piled up, almost to the ceiling, with a sheet over it. I peeped behind the sheet and saw boxes of toys with Chinese writing on them, small electric cookers that were stacked inside a child's plastic car, and then there were lots of fluffy blankets in piles, the same sort that were on the Chinese chairs. There was a door to the left of the bed, so I went through it into almost the most disgusting bathroom I'd ever seen. There was a cracked sink at one end, with no soap or towel and, at the other end, a toilet.

A toilet like I'd never seen before.

The toilet had a furry, stained, pink cover. Not just covering the lid but attached to the actual seat itself. And I do mean furry, like, mega fluffy. I looked at it, thinking, *this is the toilet of a man who just told me he's never cleaned the extrusion machine.*

There was no way I was going to put my naked butt on that fluffy seat. I would rather my bladder burst.

━━━━━

It was a frustrating first day, and we didn't feel we'd got the answers we needed about production, and we knew there were many things we wanted to try to improve. Before we could go back to our hotel to work out a plan together, we drove with Mei and Xin to a nearby town for dinner, which was in a huge hall-type building, filled with round tables with circular turntables so people could help themselves to food. There were large tanks full of live seafood at the entrance, with people pointing at what they wanted to eat.

Felix and I immediately noticed a pale-coloured sea worm that in all honesty looked like a long, flaccid penis, with an opening at one end that would open and close, I guess so it could breathe. It was wiggling around slowly in the middle of the tank, sliding around the tentacles of crustaceans and occasionally coming to the surface for air.

Obviously, this was fascinating to Felix and me and we were pointing at it, which Mei thought meant we wanted to eat the dick-worm (what is it with worms?), and we tried to assure her that we really, really didn't want it. Then we pointed at some tiny, brown-looking bony things in a kind of shiny sauce, sitting on the buffet table next to the tanks, which turned out to be duck tongues.

Our fascination backfired, because when we insisted we didn't want the dick-worm or the tongue, Mei's response was: "No need to be shy!" and she gestured to the staff to include some in our order. Felix stopped her, saying that she could order them if she wanted to eat them, but we wouldn't.

After that experience, we mainly said we were tired after our long days and would be fine to eat at the hotel.

The next day, we loaded up on as much breakfast as we could: eggs, toast, hash browns, pancakes, fruit, yoghurt and waffles and we wrapped up bagels with cream cheese and croissants with jam and put them in our bags, with a plan that we'd sneak bites out of them if we could during the day.

# 15.
# Mei and the Missing invisibobble Factory, Part Two

**WHAT I LEARNED:**

- **Visiting rural China can mean tasting all kinds of food**
- **If you have an overseas fixer, be VERY specific about their role**
- **Production is vitally important, and we needed a dedicated person to oversee it early on**

On day two of our Chinese factory visit, we went back to ask more questions and try to get answers. After the meal with Mei and Xin and our second encounter with worms and food, Felix and I went back to the hotel and wrote a long list of things we needed to explain to Xin and things we didn't understand. We hadn't got answers about how many hair ties were produced every day, and we hadn't actually seen anyone working the machine or soldering the ends of the hair ties together into a circle, because it had only been Xin there the day before.

We wanted to know this for the audits our retail customers would come and do. But we also needed the factory workers to understand the importance of getting the colours and thicknesses of the invisibobbles right and the sizes had to be exactly right so they could fit precisely into the packaging. That way, they would have a mass production feel and be consistent for all the retailers and salons that sold them and for the people putting our hair ties in their hair.

After our dawn wake-up call, we left our hotel in Qingdao, our bags stuffed with stolen breakfast goods, to get back into the car to bump along the dirt track for three hours, with our heads bumping against the windows as we snoozed. When we got to the factory it was just Xin again. The extrusion machine had been cleaned, at least, and it turned out to be silver and not black. They'd also put a bucket at one end, so the strips of unsoldered invisibobbles would no longer drop straight on to the floor.

We started going through our list, and to each question, the answer would be "OK," and not much else. So, I'd say, "Can you make sure that each invisibobble is the same thickness?" and Mei would translate. Xin would nod and give one-word answers. Then I'd say, "We need all the colours to be consistent. Can you make sure all the colours are consistent?" and get the same wide-eyed nod. Felix and I would look at each other, wide-eyed, as we took it in turns to ask questions. Then we asked more about how the invisibobbles were coiled, cut and soldered. We needed to understand how, after the long strip of coloured plastic would come out of the machine, it was cut to the right length.

After much discussion between Mei and Xin, the answer came back: "We just cut."

"But how do you make sure they are cut to the right length?" I asked.

"He says, 'We just cut,'" Mei said.

I took a deep breath.

"Can you show me how they are cut?"

That seemed to be the hardest question of all. After another long chat between Mei and Xin, he held up his hand with his fingers in a scissor shape.

"No," I said. "I'm asking you to physically show me, exactly how you cut the material into strips." I picked up a strip of invisibobble and put it down on the table.

"We, cut, like this," Mei said, as he demonstrated, with just a pair of scissors, and no ruler.

We ended up finding a ruler and drawing on the table the exact length each invisibobble needed to be. We did this several times at the table where they told us the factory workers sat, cutting the strips down to size.

These measurements seemed to take most of the morning and when it was lunchtime, they invited us to a building next door. The factory was freezing and the lunchroom was super warm, so in some ways we were happy to go there. But mainly not, because of what was on offer.

Even though we had stolen food from breakfast, we hadn't mastered the art of sneaking away to eat it, and somehow Felix decided it was my turn to be polite and pretend lunch was delicious. A plate of shiny, caramel-brown pieces of meat appeared, with bones sticking out either side. It looked fresh and was steaming hot, so I took a bite. It tasted like chicken in soy sauce – not too bad – so I nodded and smiled. If you like something, the Chinese way is to give you more of it, and another plate soon arrived. Xin smiled and said something to Mei.

"He say, 'you like braised hog foot!'" Mei said.
"Hog foot?" Felix said, enjoying every minute, as I stopped chewing.
"Yes, how you say? Pig trotter!"

I tried to smile, though I wanted to violently spit the contents of my mouth on the floor. I swallowed, making a mental note that it was Felix's turn to take one for the team next time.

We had many, many other questions that didn't get clarified that day, or the next, but Mei kept promising she would get us answers. Things like how many people worked there, the precise length of material that got extruded from the machine each day, the number of invisibobbles that got made each hour and each day, what the working hours were and how many breaks people got.

Every time we asked a detailed question about production, Mei would ask Xin, and he would answer, eventually, after much discussion. We wanted details of sizes, quantities, weights, measurements, hourly rates versus daily or monthly rates: very specific queries. We also wanted to see proof of employee contracts as well as records of workers stamping in and out every day.

After one particularly detailed question, Mei said, "No computer."

"No computer?" I said, trying to keep a straight face as I looked at Felix.

"We cannot check number on computer because Xin's grandmother has borrowed it."

Felix was standing slightly behind Mei and Xin at that point and he raised his eyebrows, then hunched over and made typing motions with his fingers. I swallowed hard, holding back a burst of laughter.

"Where does Xin's grandmother live? Can we go and collect it? We have a driver here," I said. Another long conversation between Mei and Xin ensued.

"He say, 'his cousin took computer from grandmother, and they need it for something something wedding,'" Mei said.

*Something something wedding?!*

"Wedding in two weeks, they go by boat, take computer," she said.

*Such an obvious explanation! So relieved to hear this reason,* I thought.

At that point, a noise that sounded like a high-pitched fart came out of Felix's mouth and I had to turn away, putting my hands over my eyes and pretending to sneeze. I tried to stop the laughter by turning toward the filthy stove area for a cup of grey tea, which made everything worse because Xin rushed over to pour it for me. I drank it, then laughed so hard the tea came out of my nose and I had to pretend to have caught a very sudden cold. But then a wave of frustration came over me and tears pricked in my eyes. We had travelled all the way to China to sort out our production problems and were getting NOWHERE. It just felt like they were making everything up.

"Xin say he knows all the answers, tell you numbers, you write on paper, then you have record," Mei said.

We had no choice but to agree, and slowly Xin answered our questions through Mei. But he never, not once looked at a piece of paper or in a folder to check. How could he possibly know all of these figures? Each time he told us a number, Felix would write it down, so we could do the maths later at the hotel with the grand, gold entrance and lettuce-and-bread club sandwiches.

We also hadn't seen where or how the ends of the strips got coiled and then soldered together into the final, circular invisibobble hair tie, and we hadn't even got on to packaging. Where were the invisibobbles packed into boxes of three? Who oversaw that?

Xin agreed to show us how the invisibobbles got coiled and soldered together and it came as an awful shock. The soldering place was next to the factory with the extrusion machine, and it was just a table with about six chairs around it, with these super-hot metal rods sitting on the table and people melting each end of the invisibobble on the hot rod and then holding them so they stuck together. They had no gloves and no masks, just their bare hands. We immediately insisted they get gloves and masks at least, but we later found out that this is the kind of casual job farm workers do in the evenings. They are given a soldering iron and they would solder invisibobbles from home to make some extra money. (It's a pretty skilled job – I tried soldering an invisibobble once and it took me six minutes to just do one.)

We knew we had a massive job on our hands to improve production, to make life better for the people working for the factory, and to make sure the invisibobbles were the best quality they could be.

One thing we also insisted on understanding more about was why our colours sometimes looked faded and other times came out too dark or too bright. Where did the colours get added to the plain invisibobble coils? How were they mixed and weighed? We pushed Xin and Mei to discuss this, and eventually they got the colour supplier to agree to show us where he worked.

I started imagining how the colour factory might look. I imagined rows of shelves, each one containing huge glass jars of different powdered colours all lined up, starting at the top with blacks and charcoal greys, then darkest midnight blue, through to deep green, grass green, yellow, orange, red, pink and purple. I imagined all the colours of the rainbow piled up floor to ceiling in one gorgeous, inspiring world.

The reality was, it looked like a dump.

We couldn't even see the powdered colours with all the junk that was around. A bit like the invisibobble factory, there seemed to be boxes of toys, a few mattresses, random electrical goods and rolled-up carpets. There was very little colour pigment anywhere, apart from on a small working table, which had a weighing scale on it and a few small jars.

We sat down with the manager (and this time it was Felix's turn to drink the dishwater tea), trying to explain, via Mei, how important it was to measure the colours correctly. He kept smiling and nodding, smiling and nodding. At some point, I needed the toilet, and the guy pointed to a back area. There wasn't a bathroom as such: it was more like a kind of a half-enclosed space with a curtain, where I could see a couple of buckets on the floor. I looked around for a toilet, but I couldn't see one. It was quite dark back there, and when my eyes adjusted, I realized the buckets were full of liquid. The buckets were full of piss.

For some reason, that day we decided to get the guy to take a picture of us with Mei. Looking back at the photo, Felix and I look terrible, like kids whose parents have been executed. With the shock of seeing the conditions some of the people worked in, the exhaustion of travelling, the language divide, the unfamiliar food, the filth and the lack of answers about anything, we looked pale, confused and bereft.

How were we ever going to get our factory up to the standards we needed it to be, for our own company requirements and for the retailers' audits, let alone for the Chinese people who worked there?

That night, we managed to avoid having dinner with Mei. I was desperate for normal food, and on the outskirts of Qingdao, I spotted a KFC, formally known as 'Kentucky Fried Chicken.' Fast food restaurants are not usually my thing, but a whole, sweet-smelling bucketful of hot, breaded and fried chicken seemed like the only thing I wanted to eat in the entire world at that point.

After about five minutes of conversation between the staff at the restaurant, they eventually handed us a small tub. It wasn't a bucket and there was no breaded chicken. Instead, there was a pile of chicken wings in soy sauce with rice underneath. It was definitely different than the KFC I'd had before, but I ate it.

Most toilets in China are hole-in-the-ground style, so you just squat over them, and you kind of have to get used to that. After some searching, I found the door to the toilet. Toilet, singular, you understand. But instead of it being one small, enclosed cubicle for the whole restaurant to share, I opened the door and it was a communal toilet *room*, with a row of toilet holes in the ground, no walls to separate them and both men and women doing their thing, in front of each other, at the same time.

Much as I appreciated this was normal for Chinese people, I couldn't do it. I very quickly did a 180-degree turn out of the toilet and out of the restaurant. I know that things are done differently all around the world, but this toilet situation was one of the biggest culture shocks for us.

In the end, I insisted the driver drop me off in the middle of the highway, and I jumped out of the car, ran into whatever bush I could find, dropped my pants and went by the side of the road, in the dark, not caring if people could see me or whether I got bitten by a poisonous spider.

The next day, there was more of the same at the factory with very few answers. We stole more breakfast from the hotel, rarely drank water for fear of needing the toilet, took it in turns to take tiny sips of Chinese tea and made a bit of progress in getting Mei to understand that he needed to check that all the measurements were correct every day. But we still weren't getting very far.

Because everything seemed so vague, so dirty and so unprofessional, we increasingly had the feeling we weren't being told the truth, or that other factories were involved in production.

Mei wasn't giving us answers and the whole thing seemed to amount to one big lie. We really needed to understand the entire process – which would ideally happen under one roof – so that we could have everything audited.

We started secretly recording the conversations that were being had between Mei and Xin, because after the first day when we got no answers at all and the production guy seemed to pluck numbers out of thin air, we got very suspicious. We sent the recording to a Chinese friend to translate for us, but he said the conversations were pretty basic and there didn't seem to be anything dodgy happening.

So, we tried a different tactic: we turned up at the factory unannounced one day, without Mei. The extrusion machine was switched off and there were about six Chinese workers there with boxes that they were packing full of invisibobbles ready to be shipped. It made no sense that you would convert an entire factory into a packing station overnight, so we asked what was going on and they just said that day was a packing day.

There were large bags full of invisibobble hair ties that the workers were opening and stacking into boxes. Why would they bother to pack large bags of our products only to open them up and put them into boxes? It didn't add up.

I had a closer look at the bags, and they had labels on them, all in Chinese characters. Mei said they were 'batch codes,' whatever that meant. We took a picture, and when we got back to Munich, our Chinese friend translated.

There was no batch code. It was an address in the city of Linfen, nearly 600 miles from Qingdao.

My school friend Hope always imagined she'd become an oil trader, because it was a fast-paced, male-dominated industry she thought she could stand out in, have an exciting time with and make lots of money.

She started applying for jobs, spending entire days doing fake trades on a platform the bank had set up to test potential employees, with some patronizing guy looking over her shoulder, questioning her profit margins. Hope concluded that if the test was like that – which she described as a "horrendous and intensely negative experience" – then actually working for one of those banks would probably be worse. We started chatting about her maybe coming to work for invisibobble.

Hope knew that invisibobble had become a 'thing' a few years before when we went on that trip to Barcelona and I'd spent the whole time writing invoices. Fast-forward a few years, and I'm living in Munich, Hope in London. She's British and did a masters after my degree and visited me in Germany a few times. Every time, I'd point out my favourite restaurants and say things like, "That's the kind of place I'd go for dinner on a Tuesday," and Hope would say, "Oh, nice," and then change the subject. I was subtly kind of trying to find out whether she would maybe consider moving to Munich and working for invisibobble, because she is super intelligent and detailed and has a much more logistical brain than me. I thought she could be good at operations or sales maybe.

The more I told her about the company, the more interested she became. We started talking quite freely about it. I explained that we had some salespeople, we had pretty good distribution, and we had ideas about new products we wanted to develop. But because Hope had been so much into the oil trading idea, she was worried that invisibobble had nothing to do with the skills she had, and also, she had absolutely no idea at all about the beauty industry.

I reminded her that Felix and I had absolutely no idea about the beauty industry at all when we started either, but let her know confidentially that we had turned over nearly $7 million the year before, which was only our third full year in business.

Anyway, I was in London, celebrating my 22nd birthday at a kind of fancy Chinese restaurant where we were all getting pretty drunk. I thought it would be a good idea to subtly sit Hope next to Dani (they hadn't met before), who could assess her suitability as a possible invisibobble employee. As she was my friend, I needed someone objective who could work out how she might fit. We were sitting at quite a long table: Hope and Dani were opposite me, and I was next to Felix, so I could keep half an ear on what they were discussing.

Hope has all kinds of food allergies, so had ordered a special meal that was different than what everyone else was eating. It was a duck salad and, it turns out, that was Dani's favourite dish on the menu. Hope kind of knew that she had to impress Dani, so she gave him some of her food.

Then he started firing questions at Hope about the oil industry, in great depth, because he's the kind of person who likes to go into minute detail about anything, kind of as a test to see if that person *really* knows what they are talking about. So, while Dani was eating Hope's duck salad, she was telling him everything about oil trading and I was getting super drunk on the other side of the table. Hope shoved a prawn cracker in her mouth from time to time as she carried on answering questions, and she would very occasionally glance at me as if to say *who is this guy?* I was no use because I was the birthday girl and had started doing shots, but eventually Dani left and we went to a club, where Hope could finally have a drink. It wasn't exactly a conventional interview.

Dani was pretty impressed, and we eventually agreed that Hope would come and work at invisibobble with the rough job title of 'Project Manager' on the research and development 'team.' She eventually became the head of Research and Development, but for a while there it kind of morphed into a head of production role, because we had a serious problem with production in China, and we urgently needed to sort it out.

Some years before, Hope had been to Beijing on a school singing trip where she stayed with a Chinese girl and her family. One Friday evening, when Hope went into her room, she asked the Chinese girl what she was doing that night.

"I'm watching *Grey's Anatomy*," she answered.

Hope looked around, but she couldn't see a TV, just a big, open physics textbook, which was on the girl's lap as she sat cross legged on the bed.

The Chinese girl was pretending not to work. It seemed to Hope to be a cultural thing, where some students worked very hard but would cover it up so that they could appear cool, or make it seem as if their good grades were effortless. But in actual fact, they were studying 18 hours a day to keep their parents happy. The Chinese girl's parents were super strict, and the family lived in a kind of dull, grey compound, where the girl and her sister would both practise violin for two hours a day when they weren't studying.

Hope's first impression of China was of a place that was safe, regimented and pretty dull. But that was about to change dramatically.

———

After our first trip to China, we realized we urgently needed a plan B, and Hope was going to help us. We still weren't getting answers from Mei about how our invisibobbles were made or the numbers that got produced every day or how they managed quality control (ha!). We hadn't seen any kind of written health and safety standards for staff, and we had no idea if the gloves and masks we got for the workers were still being used.

We decided we had to stop placing orders until we got answers, which meant that she was no longer paying the production facility.

A couple weeks after we stopped ordering (Mei had gone very quiet), we got an email, which went something like this: "Hi, I'm from your factory in Linfen, you haven't paid us for two weeks. What's going on?"

Linfen? We didn't have a factory there. We wrote back, in disbelief, asking for proof that they were producing invisibobbles. In return, they sent us invoices and all the paperwork we had asked Mei for, things like the exact quantities of all the products they made for us, how many they produced per day, week and month, and which salon or retail customers they were going to.

It turned out that a factory in Linfen, not Qingdao, nearly 600 miles away, had been producing invisibobbles for THREE YEARS. After multiple emails, we discovered there was more than one factory in China producing invisibobbles, which got sent to Qingdao. The Qingdao factory was used for packing only, and Mei had known about it all along, In fact, she had been the orchestrator of the whole thing.

We worked out that over the three years, Mei had outsourced the manufacturing of our hair ties to different factories, which every month would send thousands of invisibobbles by road to Qingdao, where they were packed and shipped. She would pay the Linfen factory and the others, then mark up the price of production MASSIVELY, add her own fees, and pass the cost on to us, pretending all the while that the Qingdao factory was making our products. Mei had cleverly sold her services to Felix and me, telling us she would source manufacturing for us. But it turns out she didn't actually have any direct contacts at the factories that were specialists in plastic production, and she hadn't managed the process at all, so no wonder our hair ties were sometimes funny colours or sizes.

We asked the Linfen factory how much they were charging Mei to produce invisibobbles, and the answer made me want to vomit and cry all at the same time. We worked out that Mei had overcharged us by more than $900,000 a year, and over three years, the total we had been cheated out of was £2.2 million (about $2.8 million).

I'll say that again: we had been cheated out of £2.2 million.

That is the kind of sum that could take a small company down, but I guess because invisibobbles had been selling so well, we managed to keep going. But even so, we were completely furious, and of course we took Mei to court.

But we lost.

We lost the case because the judge could not accept the difference between Mei sourcing from a factory direct and managing the production process, as she had told us she did, and her outsourcing the whole production process to several other, random factories, and then all she did was manage packaging and shipping in Qingdao. She had told so many lies. We were angry and devastated, but we had to move on.

# 16.

# The Yellow Hair Girl and the Orange Hair Girl

**WHAT I LEARNED:**

- Chickens can cross factory lines
- It's nearly impossible to manufacture plastic products at scale outside China
- 'Saving face' is a thing in China, and it's very hard to deal with

After the disaster with Mei, we needed to work out exactly which factory in Linfen was making invisibobbles, but we knew we needed to look at alternatives too. It's always good to get to know the market – who manufactures what, how much they charge and so on – and because we had relied so heavily on Mei, we had no idea what our options were. That was Hope's first job, and I joined her on a road trip to find out.

Hope and I know each other so well that we can almost read each others' minds, even from the tiniest twitch of the mouth or slightly raised eyebrow, and in China we developed a way to communicate without speaking. A tiny cock of the head means

"Meet me in the toilet so we can talk," and although we know how much I hate Chinese factory toilets, they were pretty much the only places we could have a conversation.

As we know, there is fake everything in China, and Hope and I would end up trying to find the items that made us laugh the most. One of my favourites is a sweater with 'Ballinciaga' printed on it (Balenciaga is a Spanish luxury fashion brand) and I now keep that in my suitcase of clothes I only wear in China.

I am tall (in China), with long, straight blonde hair, and Hope is a redhead with lots of freckles, and aside from people staring at us wherever we went, they also started to take photos. Remember, we're still in rural China and far, far from cities, so it's unlikely the people we encountered had seen many Westerners before, let alone two women who must have looked strange to them.

It wasn't just the factory managers who'd take photos, but the people on the production lines who would stop what they were doing, pick up their phones and point them at us, without asking. It got to the point where we would put our hair up in ponytails and wear caps, as well as our baggy Ballinciaga sweaters, just so we would attract less attention. But because in China you might know someone whose cousin's wife's dog knows someone else in a factory on the other side of the country, the photos people took of us somehow spread around to different parts of China, to different factories and producers, and somehow they would work out that we were from invisibobble.

Remember, we had started sourcing our products on Alibaba. I'd often get messages with some Chinese person trying to sell a lid for a jar, or a case for your bra, random stuff like that and about two weeks after that trip I got an email via the website, which went something like: "Hi. We see you yellow hair girl and orange hair girl go in China factory, look for producer. We can be producer. Contact now!"

I got several more of those kinds of emails, which I ignored. God knows how many people's phones have pictures of me and Hope on them.

The yellow hair girl and the orange hair girl went to all kinds of hair accessories factories, being picked up by a taxi at 5am and driving down various bumpy dirt road tracks and around boulders in the middle of the road for interminable amounts of time. Each factory visit got more and more disappointing and sometimes shocking.

During our travels, we even saw a couple of factories that manufactured spiral hair ties for big European retailers. As I already explained, it's pretty standard practice for stores to make their own versions of branded things and some of the retailers we supplied with invisibobble started making their own label spiral hair ties, the kind they'd staple to a piece of cardboard and sell just like regular elastic hair ties. It was weird seeing those factories, but we had to accept it was a fact of life that because our product had done well, retailers started to make their own versions.

A lot of the time we'd find extrusion machines similar to the one at the Qingdao factory, just sitting there without being used, and we'd ask why they were dormant. The factory managers would say they weren't extruding that day, but we got the feeling that they never did, that the machines were just for show, and they'd source products from other parts of the country and just pack them there. But the factory managers never wanted to tell us the truth because of the Chinese culture of wanting to 'save face.'

We use a material called TPU, which has particular properties when you heat it, and it means that you can put an invisibobble into hot water and it will go back to its original shape if it has stretched. There's also PU, which does not shrink back in boiling water – it just stays stretched. In one factory, there were bags labelled PU everywhere, and I asked the manager what material they manufactured with.

"TPU," she said.

"Oh really? Why are there bags all over the place labelled 'PU'?" I said.

"Those are not PU bags," she said.

"But it says PU on there," I said.

"We took the TPU bag of products, emptied it and filled a PU bag."

This was one of many WTF moments, where we would ask straightforward questions and get very cloudy, strange, made-up answers. I may as well have been asking a grape questions, for all the truth I got.

In another factory, we saw the usual machinery, which was on the left-hand side of a long building, and there was a load of chewed-up corn husks all over the floor.

"Why is there so much corn on the floor?" Hope asked the guy showing us around.

"For chickens," he said. *Chickens. Of course, the chickens. A spiral hair tie factory with chickens. Sure.*

"Chickens? Why do you have chickens in the factory?"

"No chickens in factory!" the guy said angrily.

But there they were, about 12 chickens, clucking around on the floor, right in front of our faces. Some of them had massive bald patches or hardly any feathers at all and they were pecking about and running in all directions.

"But I can see the chickens running about, here!"

"Factory stop here!" He pointed along an invisible line in the middle of the long room.

*Of course. That half is for the chickens and this is half is the factory, silly us,* Hope thought, and looked at me. I was trying to stop myself from choking with shock and laughter.

But then we saw the area where the spiral hair ties were being soldered. It was way, way worse than any poultry running around.

There were seven or eight women, sitting at a table soldering the ends of the hair ties together. But they had no gloves or masks, and to make it much, much more awful, some of them had babies on their laps, who were moving their little arms and legs around, inches from the hot soldering irons.

There was no way we would ever, ever use this factory, and I screamed at the manager that he was risking people's lives. He shouted something back at me in Chinese and raised his fist. We had to get out of there.

Later on, during the same trip, we visited a massive factory that made hair grips, also known as bobby pins, because we had an idea that we could make an invisibobble version without metal (more on this later). The factory probably makes something like 60% of the world's bobby pins, and I had read that it was certified by a renowned auditing company, which means it was recognized for having certain quality and safety standards. So, my hopes were really high, and I was imagining that it would be the largest and most efficient factory I'd seen in my entire life.

It all started well, because we walked into a proper meeting room, where they proudly displayed all the logos of the companies they made hair grips for, and our guy spoke some English. They showed us samples of everything they made and then we asked to see the production line. I was excited because I was expecting to see a massive machine, maybe 25 metres long, that would stretch the metal so it could be bent into shape. I thought we'd see thousands of pins coming out of it every minute, then going through the paint machines so they'd come out different colours.

Then there would be lots of people sorting and packing them, before they were shipped to almost every country in the world.

But the factory managers tried to put us off, saying the machines were being cleaned, and they would be able to answer any questions we had there in the office. But we pushed them, saying that if we were going to make any products with them, we needed to be able to see the production. One of them made a phone call in Chinese, and then hung up and said the machines had finished being cleaned and it was OK if we wanted to have a look.

We walked into this huge, high-ceilinged hall, which was pretty much the largest factory I'd ever seen, with huge pieces of equipment. But it was strangely quiet, and at the far end of this huge hall, I could just about see a glum-looking woman sitting on a chair holding a small plastic bag at the end of a conveyor belt. Three pins were travelling along the belt, and she picked them up and put them in the bag, and into a cardboard box on her lap. Then she waited about a minute for the next lot.

That was it. There was no one else in the entire factory, the factory that made most of the world's supply of bobby pins.

Hope asked where everyone else was.

"On their lunch break."

"OK, we're happy to wait until they come back," she said.

"Actually, most of them have the day off today," the factory guy said.

"OK, we'll come back tomorrow," Hope said.

"It's OK, you have the paperwork, you've seen our standards, you don't need to come back," came the answer.

Again, we weren't getting anywhere, and nothing made sense. They were pretty much saying, "Either you want to manufacture here or you don't. You've seen the document that says we are up to ISO standards, now leave and stop being a pain in the ass."

But we pushed and pushed them, asking more and more questions. We got answers ranging from, "We don't have any orders to fulfil at the moment" to "We had to stop the machines running this week because my cousin is ill and the factory staff need to look after his pet pigeon" or "My grandmother needed to borrow the computer that runs the factory."

We started playing hardball and finally said we didn't believe them, and that we wouldn't leave until we had answers.

Eventually, they told us the truth.

The production line they showed us only made samples.

It wasn't the real factory; so in other words, whoever had ticked the boxes and done the paperwork had done so for what was effectively a fake factory. It was a pretend factory they used for auditing, and we discovered they had three other production sites, and when we asked to see them, the factory manager said no, because they were "really bad." We left, depressed and defeated. We had high hopes for this factory and desperately wanted to find reassurance that there would be somewhere in China that treated people fairly, but we just found lies and cover-ups.

We were also saddened by the fact that the discovery of this sample production line meant that massive multinational companies were basically turning a blind eye to how some Chinese factory workers were treated. Their 'audits' were just box-ticking exercises. What was also frustrating was the fact that larger companies often insisted that smaller companies like us were actually properly audited, which is quite hypocritical.

The reason people manufacture certain products in China is its cost-effectiveness and because the Chinese have decades of expertise in taking raw materials and making them into different types of plastic and then manufacturing at scale. No other country can really match that.

We saw this on a massive scale when we went to Yiwu, which has the largest small-commodity wholesale market in the world. We realized on the plane that there was going to be something different about the place, because of the variety of nationalities flying into the city and collecting massive empty suitcases from the baggage carousels.

The market itself has more than 75,000 stores on several levels, selling everything you've ever seen in souvenir shops abroad, from Turkish blue eye charms to Greek column fridge magnets, wooden Hindu buddhas and plastic Statues of Liberty. The factories around the market produce about 60% of the world's Christmas decorations and the market itself was just an overwhelmingly large, noisy, not very clean place that made me feel kind of depressed. People go on holiday and think they've bought something authentic, but chances are it came from this market.

We have also spent a long time trying to manufacture invisi-bobbles in Europe, but the expertise with raw materials, as well as the speed of production, just isn't there, and people simply don't want to, and won't, work on production lines soldering hair ties. It's a different story with some of our other products that are made with injection moulding, which can all be done by a machine and they don't need finishing by hand, so we can make those in Germany.

---

Toward the end of that road trip, we got a sense of which factories really made stuff and which didn't. Little things like "Employee of the Month" notices made us feel like they were actual producers who cared about their employees.

On pretty much our last day, we walked into a factory in Linfen and knew that it was The One. It was a really surreal experience. After all the stuff with Mei and the fake factory, and with all the terrible conditions we'd seen people working in, we almost didn't believe we'd find the true source. But we walked in and just like that, there were our bags of invisibobbles all labelled with colours and batch codes, neatly stacked and ready to go. We were still cautious and questioned everything they said, but we agreed to do a test delivery directly from them, and it worked fine.

Hope checked that all the workers there had contracts, were paid a fair salary and had good toilet facilities and rest areas. She made sure there were proper fire procedures, as well as employing someone to check safety standards, and that is the factory we still produce from. Now we have a guy on the ground who we trust to help us with everything, and he knows we like evidence and hate lies.

The next cultural chasm we had to try and cross was a lot easier, but had its own challenges: America.

# 17.
# Disaster of the Day

20 MILLION INVISIBOBBLES SOLD

**WHAT I LEARNED:**

- **If you are going to move products by boat, get insurance that covers EVERYTHING**
- **Discounting is the worst**
- **Keep some separation between work and your personal life**

The year 2015 turned out to be the year we christened a new business term: Disaster of the Day. We even created a shorthand for it: D.O.D. Even though we'd had our factory destroyed by a typhoon and our products ripped off (several times), they were only two of the several bad things to happen to us.

During that summer, Felix had been pushing us to stop flying invisibobbles from the factory in China to our warehouse in Munich, because of the amount of money it was costing us. Shipping products isn't particularly simple, however. You can put one pallet on a boat, but it doesn't actually save much money, and you really need to be sending massive quantities by sea to make it cost efficient.

Having invisibobbles travel by boat is nerve-wracking, as they are locked in a ship for eight to ten weeks, which was tricky for us when we were in the middle of such a big growth phase and salons and retailers wanted their products quickly. But it got to the point where we had enough orders that we could fill half a shipping container with packs of invisibobbles: 400,000 packs of three, so 1.2 million hair ties in total. A shipload, or a shitload, in other words.

We had produced a new summer collection of colours that year, so they needed to get over to Europe quickly so they could get into stores while it was still actually summer, and this is what made up most of our half container. We hadn't had any updates on where exactly the ship was, but we knew the date it was due in Hamburg. The date came and went, and there was no ship, and no notice of where it was.

One day, Hope got an email, subject line: "Whoops the boat set on fire and now it's been seized off the coast of Somalia."

It was a disaster.

That was pretty much all we got. Then another email came through: "We can't open any of the containers because of the risk of toxic fumes."

Then another: "We have managed to open the container and your products are intact."

*Phew!*

And finally: "You need to do a toxicity test when you get the products just in case."

That seemed reasonable.

When we got the shipment, Hope and I rushed to our warehouse outside Munich. The invisibobbles were definitely not intact. The packaging had partially melted, but the weirdest thing ever, which to this day I cannot explain, was that some of the invisibobbles seemed to have evaporated. Instead of three in a pack, there was one and a half, with the half stuck to the bottom of the packaging. Most of the packs were destroyed.

*But we have insurance!* I thought. I checked our insurance.

We weren't covered for fire.

Of course we weren't, because we had no idea that a ship setting on fire would be a thing. (Afterwards, we paid for a bond and managed to get a few thousand dollars back, but it took years to come through.)

We had to fly in a load more invisibobbles to make up for the 400,000 packs, which had a retail value of about £2.5 million (around $3.2 million). Again, this could have killed our business, but we were just about OK because we had been selling well. But it is another example of how, even in 2015, we were still kids trying to make a go of our business. We had this combination of naivety and real drive to make invisibobble work in the long term.

Around the time we were sorting out our production in China, we also realized that sales in our existing markets had started to decline, and our distributors were telling us that it was because invisibobbles were just a fad. We were adding new countries all the time, and they were making up for our lost sales, but that stabilization can never be the goal – there has to be growth. As well as copies coming onto the market, we had a huge problem with pricing in some regions.

When a retailer puts products on its shelves, it ultimately decides how much to sell them for. A product manufacturer can only give a recommended retail price, or RRP (in the US it's manufacturer's suggested retail price, or MSRP), but the retailer has no legal obligation to sell your products at that price. We negotiate with retailers as much as we can to avoid discounting, because once you get into that game, it damages the brand and turns products into a cheap commodity just like any other hair tie.

We noticed that retailers that were serviced by one particular Danish distributor hadn't been taking enough care that the products were being sold at their true value. We pushed her to make sure invisibobble was sold at full price, but the discounting continued. Eventually, we had to play hardball with her and cancelled our contract. But then the distributor made her own copies and sold them to salons in Denmark, where she was based. So, we got another distributor, who was based in Finland, and now we are very strong there but less so in Denmark.

It's kind of a balance: you play hard with distributors and retailers over price. If you pull your contract but the product is still important to them, you risk them making copies. Discounting is no good for brand building and it gets even more complicated when selling on something like Amazon, which I think most manufacturers have a love-hate relationship with. (See chapter 24 for more on Amazon.)

In among the Chinese factory issues, the ship setting on fire, the declining sales, the copies, and the discounting in 2015, there was another issue going on. Felix and I were great partners in the company, and from the start we had worked on invisibobble together, read every email together, packed boxes of hair ties just the two of us and spent almost every waking moment building the brand. We'd had so many experiences from packing that bloody pallet to dealing with the typhoon in China and sorting out the disasters of the day. We had poured all our love into invisibobble and each other.

I had dealt with Felix's moods, like the time he got so angry he threw his phone headset across the room and it smashed into hundreds of tiny pieces that I then, silently, picked up by hand, digging them out of the fluffy carpet and putting them back on his desk.

Felix had learned that my instinct about the brand was often right. He had agreed to putting Candy Pink and Crystal Clear invisibobbles into production, trusting me that they would sell, even though he thought that eight different colours was way too many. And even though he had told me to pull myself together that lonely afternoon when I was in the library at Warwick, when I felt like I was on the edge of a breakdown, I respected him for making me push through one of the toughest times I've had.

To this day he'll call me ten times in 12 hours to get updates on how a deal is going with a retailer; not because he thinks I can't handle it, but because he cares so much about the brand. Believe me, he's an amazing businessman.

And although we argued sometimes, Felix and I had got to the point where he started running finance and operations and I was in charge of the brand and creative ideas. We knew the parts of the business we were best at and trusted each other to get on with them. Our roles became separate, and we were spending so much time on the business, we didn't have a lot of time for our relationship. We had started dating aged 16, and by 2015, we had been together for seven years. But as things progressed at invisibobble, they kind of regressed between us. I guess we were so focused on the business, we forgot about 'us.' And so, one sunny Sunday in Munich, Felix came over to my apartment, and we decided to break up. It was kind of a personal D.O.D for both of us, and we were really sad about it, but we knew it was for the best.

I couldn't bear the thought of going to work on Monday and having to sit in the office all day with Felix around, so I booked a flight to Spain to see my mum for a week. I hadn't planned on taking any time off that summer, but that trip became my holiday. When I returned to the office, Felix was on his summer break for two weeks. When we were both finally back in Munich, I felt much calmer. We had talked about whether our split would mean one of us had to leave the business, but we were having too much fun running invisibobble and neither of us wanted to give it up. We decided that we were grown-up enough to carry on working together.

By 2015, we had started hiring people (which is tough in itself), and we had about 20 staff, from a warehouse manager to an accounts person, people who helped Hope on the production team, plus a couple of marketing people. It was common knowledge that Felix and I were together, but we didn't make any kind of announcement that we'd split up. We were building a team, and the last thing we wanted was for people to lose faith in us or the company.

We hid it for a while, but inevitably, it came out. One time we were on a sales trip and when I met Zelda in our hotel lobby, she asked where Felix was.

"I guess he's taking a nap," I shrugged.
"Didn't you just leave him in your room?" she said.

Then the penny dropped.

"Ah. You're not together anymore."

It had been about six months since we'd split, and we'd managed to keep it quiet. People often ask how we managed to run the business while we were dating and then after we broke up, but I think it's a case of thinking about the bigger picture and keeping your private life separate from work.

I've always thought it strange that you could go from having this other person in your life who you share everything with, including a bed, and then suddenly you go from that to not speaking to the person ever again. So, for us, it's really nice that as a result of having this relationship, we've created this brand, this company, from nothing, and it's a business we can hopefully benefit from for the rest of our lives.

# 18.

# Three in
# a Bed

**WHAT I LEARNED:**

- **Americans may say you're awesome, but they don't always mean it**
- **When entering a new market, work with experts**
- **The fakers get EVERYWHERE**

Everyone told us we were crazy to even think about touching the United States. We started having conversations about starting to sell there in 2014, and we wanted to do it because it's such a massive market and therefore a huge opportunity.

But people told us it was a terrible idea because it's a litigious place. Someone could swallow an invisibobble on purpose or choke themselves with one and then try to sue us. They said that the brand was too European in how it looked and in terms of how we marketed ourselves, or they told us that Americans only dealt with other Americans.

There are more than 300 million people in the USA, served by some of the largest mass retailers in the world. Hair and beauty products are sold in supermarkets, high-end department stores, upscale beauty chains and specialists. One of the ways to reach buyers is via trade shows, specifically the Las Vegas edition of Cosmoprof, a smaller version of the Bologna event.

In July 2015, Felix and I flew straight to LA after one of our Chinese factory visits, and from there to Las Vegas where we met Dani, who had arrived from Munich. It turned out that only one room had been booked for the three of us, so we had to share one large, sweaty bed in a giant Vegas hotel where we rarely knew whether it was night or day because all the bright lights make out like it's constantly daytime and the building is so huge it kind of hums through the night with constant noise. This wasn't ideal for our jetlag, and I woke up sandwiched between my now ex-boyfriend Felix and his brother Dani. I spent a moment trying to work out which brother I would have to straddle when trying to get out of bed, but quickly gave up, and went for a kind of shimmy down the centre, under the duvet and onto the floor.

I went to the bathroom and looked in the mirror. I thought to myself: *I am a grown-up woman. I am the founder of a successful business and this is invisibobble's professional entry into the United States of America. Yes!*

My reflection told a different story. It was 5am. I was the jetlagged and exhausted founder of a business that had suffered several D.O.D.s and here I was wearing a fake designer t-shirt and having to share a bed with two sweaty men, not knowing whether we would make it in the US or whether I could even bear to stand up for ten minutes more, let alone the ten hours the trade show would require.

I woke up the boys and we headed for the convention centre to set up our booth. It was pretty similar to the Bologna fair, but smaller, and we often got a similar reaction from people: where's the grown-up?

Once people started talking to us, their reactions ranged from "Awesome!" or "Soooo cool!" to "Your brand is IN-CREDIBLE!" and "You guys are so great." After three days of this, my face ached from all the smiling (and my head hurt from all the vodka tonics we drank each night).

The Americans were sooooo keen about invisibobble, and we flew back to Munich super pumped by their awesome reactions and thinking: *Yeah, after this, we can just put our feet up and retire early.* We sat back and waited for the meeting requests to come flooding in.

But we got zero follow-ups.

It turned out to be the least successful trade show we had ever done. Absolutely nothing came of it, not one email or call.

So, we tried another tack. Someone had advised us to go in with an American partner who could help us launch, and we found a distributor that seemed like the right fit because they had an audience of hairdressers and were very active on social media.

We naively thought we could just send the stock to them, let them run the show, then sit back and get rich. We thought very, very wrong. In the first year of working with them, they only sold about £17,000 (around $22,000) worth of stock, which was a tiny amount considering how vast the US is. So, we started asking questions and tried to find out what was going on, and realized that no one at the company was really responsible for invisibobble. It was just one of many products they were distributing and because their expertise was in their magazine and online community, they didn't really know how to sell products to salons.

Everything happened very slowly, and we'd release a new product or special collection only for it to take months to get to stores or salons and finally into consumers' hands. We felt totally out of control with what was happening, and it gave all of us sleepless nights. Invisibobble going to America wasn't working.

It got worse. In the middle of all of this, we discovered we were being copied in the US. The rip-offs I mentioned before were mainly in Europe and, as I said, we had import seizures put on them in that region, but we weren't doing much to protect our brand on the other side of the Atlantic.

I had often searched online to see what happened when someone typed in 'invisibobble USA' or 'spiral hair tie America,' and to start with, the results came up under the website of the high-end store we were selling at. But then one day, a product that looked very much like invisibobble, but with a different name, came up, and it had very similar packaging and product claims to ours.

There was a link to a video on YouTube, so I clicked on it. A guy I'd never seen before was demonstrating his spiral hair tie at a trade show, claiming to be the inventor of this revolutionary hair bobble that was kind to hair, and directing people to a US website. There were hair ties in all different colours at his stand, and a model demonstrating putting the hair tie in her hair, and then pulling it out again with no kinks.

The hair tie also had its own website, and it was very similar to ours. Invisibobble is 'the traceless hair ring' and this brand claimed to be 'the markless hair loop.'

Who was behind this?

It didn't take long to find out the name of the founder, and his surname seemed familiar. I called Felix, who was travelling.

"I have another potential D.O.D," I said.

Down the line I could hear him laughing. We had got so used to the disasters that they had become funny, and as we had dealt with many unexpected events, it almost became a game to guess what the next one would be.

"Don't tell me. Another uninsurable weather event? A fake factory?" Felix said.

"Not this time. An American faker," I said.

Felix sighed. "Who?"

"There is this hairdresser in the US who just happens to have created a hair tie that looks very similar to invisibobble, claiming that it's kind to hair."

The guy in the video was some smooth-talking grown-up man who clearly loved the sound of his own voice, especially when he was talking about OUR product claims.

"Oh. My. God," Felix said at the end of the phone, when I sent him the video link. "Just as we are trying to get into the US!"

I hung up and looked at the video again, feeling like I was about to explode. This was a whole new level of copying. Another of those lazy old guys who had nothing better to do with his life than copy a bunch of kids and then claim the idea for himself. I was actually embarrassed for him.

It even got to the point where some people in America would ask us why invisibobble had copied this brand, not the other way around, and I had to explain that we've existed since 2011. But you learn not to get emotional about copies unless they impact sales.

That brand still exists, but isn't widely available and doesn't have a lot of social media followers. I think it's a classic case of someone seeing the product and thinking they could easily create their own version, not realizing the effort and love it takes to make a brilliant product and brand first of all, and then relentlessly find new distributors and retailers to sell it and maintain those relationships.

After we had dipped our toes into the American market without much success, we soon realized that, to somewhat paraphrase Frank Sinatra, if we were to make it there, we would have to make a massive effort.

Even though 2015 was a shit show in many ways, it was also the year I finally felt, for the first time, that invisibobble was here to stay. Our sales had been flattening out, but once we had sorted out the Chinese production, I knew we could grow. In spite of the problems, in 2015, our turnover more than doubled and I calculated that by the end of that year, one in three German women had bought an invisibobble.

We had also hired Hope, who became our head of new product development, a role that was much needed. Doing so also helped us work out the kind of people we wanted to recruit. Coming up with ideas for new products is often done by specialists: super-geeky intelligent people who might be engineers or scientists working in a lab. But we've found it works better to hire generalists, because they can often think about the bigger picture and the overall goal of a company. When Hope started, it meant that Felix and I had time to start thinking longer-term, and it also made us get more organized.

# 19.

# What I Traded 1,350 Vodka Red Bulls in For

**WHAT I LEARNED:**

- **You can convey serious messages about business in a lighthearted way**
- **An audience of eight-year-olds is a great way to practise a big speech**
- **Breathing out fully and loudly to a wall is some people's way of preparing for a presentation**

Being backstage before I gave a TEDx talk was a bit like being a jelly bean that has escaped from an overflowing handful and is now lying on the floor waiting for someone to tread on it.

Well, it was for me anyway.

In November 2015, the Copenhagen School of Design and Technology, known as KEA, had shortlisted me to do a TEDx talk. I hadn't believed they were serious when they'd sent me a casual email about six months before, asking if I'd like to pitch a speech about invisibobble.

If you haven't heard of TED before (it stands for Technology, Entertainment, Design and TEDx is a licensed version of it), here's how it works: People speak for between ten to 18 minutes and the audience is supposed to leave having learned something inspiring. Talks are then uploaded onto YouTube and stay there for eternity.

Some of the world's top entrepreneurs and thinkers have done TED talks, including magician David Blaine, who revealed how he held his breath for 17 minutes; research professor Brené Brown, who discussed the power of vulnerability; and psychologist Robert Waldinger, who explored what makes humans happy. The most-viewed TED talk ever is Sir Ken Robinson's 'Do Schools Kill Creativity?' which has been viewed more than 56 million times.

Most TED talks have titles that include powerful words and phrases like 'Extraordinary,' 'Extreme Productivity' and 'Save The World.' Their headings promise to 'Change Your Life,' 'Cultivate Unconditional Self-Worth' or make you 'Lose Weight Forever.'

My TEDx talk was called: "What I Traded 1,350 Vodka Red Bulls in For."

That's because we invested the money we saved by not drinking into invisibobble, and this title seemed like a catchy way to get people interested in my story.

I hadn't done public speaking of the magnitude of TED before, and I definitely hadn't videoed any speeches. I wanted to show memes in my talk and photos of me drunk on nights out at Warwick University (I'd graduated the year before). I wasn't trying to change the world and it didn't seem very TED.

At the TEDx pitch meeting, the guys interviewing me seemed unconvinced by the title. But I knew I had three things people would learn from my talk, very simple advice that the audience of students, CEOs and company founders could easily remember. I'll come back to the three things, but in the meeting, the only way I knew how to convince the Copenhagen team was to tell them they should have faith in me.

"The only thing I can offer you is trust," I told them.

"Trust in me that I will stand on stage and won't go blank. I will stand on stage and do my thing and it will be a proper speech."

To convince them, I had to write out the whole talk for them, which – in between all my other work – took about three weeks. Within 24 hours I got a reply: "We would officially like to welcome you to speak at TEDx KEA."

*Wow. I'm really doing this*, I thought.

I then spent hours in front of the mirror monitoring my arm movements, practising the talk with my dad and rehearsing it in front of a live audience of eight-year-olds at the junior school I went to. The eight-year-olds seemed to like it, so I figured, how bad could it be?

A couple days before the talk, I arrived alone in Copenhagen to prepare.

When I have a speech, I like to be ready at least 24 hours ahead of time, so I know that for the whole day before I can have the luxury of a completely clear mind. In Copenhagen, I was happy to stay in the hotel on my own, have dinner by myself and wander around the city streets and harbour listening to The Black Eyed Peas on my headphones.

Walking from the hotel to the rehearsal the day before my talk, I turned a corner and saw the building where it would take place. It is known as the Black Diamond, a massive, shiny, dark, glass box on the city's harbour, housing the Royal Danish Library. It's where philosopher Søren Kierkegaard's manuscripts are kept, a guy who was probably one of the cleverest humans on the planet.

I went inside and saw that the auditorium itself was really, really cool as well. And I'm thinking: *This is all too fancy for what I had in mind.*

The morning of the talk I sat on my hotel bed. My mind was blank. All I could focus on was putting on my socks.

Here's one sock, OK, it's on my foot. Now the next. I put a hair tie in my hair. I took it out. Eventually, I walked to the Black Diamond to join my parents, Felix and a few others toward the back of the auditorium. I watched three speeches and I wasn't nervous.

And then without saying anything, I left and went backstage.

There was a guy going through his talk with A4 sheets of paper that he was flicking back and forth. There was another guy in the corner breathing in and out fully and loudly toward the wall. *Ha*, he went, as he breathed out. And near me was a woman having her makeup done while she talked to a speech coach (a coach?!). The coach said, "And then what are you gonna say? And how are you going to say it? And how do you feel now? We need more power! Now rest. Let's have three minutes' silence."

All of them had an *entourage*. I had nothing. No phone, no notes, nowhere to sit. One of the backstage guys came up to me and asked, where's my accompaniment? *Accompaniment? Do I need an accompaniment?*

For something to do I flicked through the titles of the other talks: "How to Avoid Food Waste Traps," "How to Monetize Big Data," "A Manifesto of Empowerment to My Future Daughter." *I'm literally going to be talking about plastic hair ties and all the vodka tonics I may or may not have drunk at university. Fabulous.*

And that is when I started getting really nervous. I saw a bunch of chairs piled up against the wall, so I jumped up on one of the stacks. The TEDx makeup artist came over and put on foundation, mascara and eyeshadow. There was no mirror, so I didn't even know if I looked like myself or not.

While she added blusher, I decided I should go through my talk in my head. *When I was 18 years old, I decided to start a com ...*

"Sophieyou'renextonstagecomehereplease we'reputtingonyour-microphonenow," a voice said. *What?*

"Sophie, you're next on stage. Come here, please, we're putting your microphone on now."

The stage manager handed me a glass of water and attached a mic while he told me there were three steps up to the stage, and that the presentation clicker would be on the table where I will put the glass of water down.

I heard her words, and I snapped back into reality. *I can do this.*

I walked up the steps, across the stage, put the water down, picked up the clicker and stood on the big, red TEDx spot. I heard applause, although I couldn't see anyone because the stage lights were so bright. I started to speak.

Thirteen and a half minutes later, it was done. Nothing had gone wrong. As I left the stage, people kept clapping. I was shown through a door and someone took off the mic, which was complicated because I was wearing a jumper with giant batwing superman sleeves. I was so excited I wanted to down shots, hug my family and dance like no one's watching, all at the same time.

But I had to wait. I had to wait because someone else's talk had started and I was in the grand hallway of the Black Diamond on my own. There was a big window looking out over the waterfront, and I noticed it was snowing. It was completely silent, a moment of calm when my mind had been SO LOUD for so many hours.

And as I watched the snow, the door opened behind me and it was my dad's friend, who'd been watching my talk.

And he handed me my favourite drink: a vodka tonic.

# 20.
# We Are Just Behind the Poo Drops

36 MILLION INVISIBOBBLES SOLD

**WHAT I LEARNED:**

- **Guacamole stains pillows**
- **Retail negotiations are harder in the US than in Europe**
- **Being a founder can mean getting emotional about your brand**

Our American dreams had been dented, but I was still convinced we could make it work in a big way.

By the end of 2015, we did get listings in a couple of smaller retail chains over there, but there was much, much more we could do.

There were echoes in my mind of people telling us we couldn't make it in America and I still felt sore from the American faker, but then the opportunity to go to a New York trade show came up in 2016. Hope and I headed out there and it ended up being an amazing trip, partly because we found some new packaging suppliers that would help us be more cost efficient but also because we were 23 year olds doing business in the Big Apple.

We asked friends for hotel recommendations, and they suggested somewhere near the Meatpacking District that used to be a parking garage. It might have been a great place for margaritas by the rooftop pool on a Friday night, but the room was so small there was barely room for both of us, the bed (a mattress on the floor) and two suitcases. New York doesn't really do twin beds, so Hope and I shared a double, with our cases piled up by the side, and each night we'd have to kind of dive bomb onto it to avoid the debris around us. There was also nowhere to sit, so if we needed to get out of each other's way, one of us would have to perch on the toilet. Even though we travelled a lot, we always stuck to a $200-a night budget and finding a hotel room for that price in Manhattan isn't easy. In fact, $220 bought us a micro bedroom in a hip hotel where we could pass out after long days of work and longer nights of partying.

At that time, Hope and I were going through a huge Mexican phase, eating tacos for lunch, buying Mexican blankets and attempting to make our own mezcal cocktails back home in Munich. It was funny, because when we were in New York it was Cinco de Mayo, a massive fiesta that commemorates the Mexicans winning a battle over the French in 1862. We were constantly on the lookout for guacamole, and halfway through our trip, we were in a cab after a night out when we went past the sign of our dreams: 24-Hour Fajitas. There it was, blinking tastily at us through the window of the taxi.

We got back to the hotel with the biggest drunken munchies you can imagine, and we HAD to have some guac. It was 2am and the hotel's kitchen was closed, but this being New York, the fajita place would deliver at all hours. So, the receptionist got them on the line.

"Hi, can I get two fajitas with extra guacamole please?" I shouted down the phone (we had been to a LOUD bar).

"Fajitas, how? You want chicken, beef, shrimp, veg, tofu, tempeh, pork, tuna, seabass, Mexican rice, black beans, pinto beans, flageolet beans, full-fat cheese, non-fat cheese, sour cream, chilli, tomato, raw onion …" the guy said, in that American way where they list a million things in a fast monotone.

"Guaca –" I started to say.

Hope grabbed the phone.

"Hi. My name is Hope. We just want two large beef fajitas with extra guacamole, please. Is that clear?" she said, in her best drunken British accent, which out loud sounded like: "Faar-heetars wuth gwaaacaamow-lay," at that time of night.

Up in our room, we tried to sober up so we could appreciate the deliciousness of all that gwaaac. There was a knock at the door.

"24-Hour Fajitas," a guy's voice said.

Hope and I pushed each other out of the way, and I tried to grab the bag of food.

"That's 35 bucks."

I handed him my card.

"Sorry ma'am, no plastic. Cash only."
"Can we pay you in the morning?"
"No, ma'am."
"Can I give you my phone as security that we will come right away in the morning and pay? Please?" Hope said over my shoulder.

"No, ma'am."

Then a security guy appeared as a result of our drunken shouting down the hotel hallway.

"What's the problem here?"
"We need to pay for the guac, but he doesn't take cards," I explained.
"OK, sir, I'm going to have to ask you to leave with the guac," the security guy said to the 24-Hour Fajitas guy.

Hope pushed past me.

"We neeeeeed our gwaaacaamow-lay!"

Then the reception guy appeared, the one who had ordered for us. He got out his wallet.

"How much?"

The reception guy paid the guacamole guy with his own money.

Because our room was so small, the bed was the only place we could actually eat our $35-worth of guac. So we dive-bombed onto it and we lay on our bellies, holding our cardboard trays of food with one hand and stuffing our faces with the other, our bodies snaked over either side of the bed so as not to drop guac on our duvets. Then we fell asleep with our heads almost in the guac.

In the morning, I obviously woke up with a large, green stain on my pillow, and a cardboard container of tortilla chips next to my head, and of course we completely forgot that the guy at reception had paid for our fajita feast (he reminded us). We'd had about three hours' sleep. The entire week was a bit like that, with us running on margaritas, guacamole and giant Starbucks, either drunk or hungover, but mostly having a ball.

It was also the first time I'd met journalists in the US. We had a PR agency who introduced me to magazine editors and writers, without telling me much about what they were keen to hear about. We got some pretty good write-ups from that, but as with most things, I was in the dark on how it actually worked. At that time, I'd launch into "Hi, I'm Sophie, these are our invisibobble hair ties, they don't mark your hair," but now I at least find out what the journalist is interested in writing about before I meet them.

At the end of the week, I flew to Chicago for a meeting with our head of sales, Zelda, and one of the largest salon distributors in the US. My flight was delayed, and I arrived at my hotel at about 2.30am, took an extended nap, and woke up at 5.30am to get to the meeting. I'd kind of assumed that Zelda had done the maths and worked out how much we needed to sell to the distributor, and what collections we hoped they'd buy from us, but she hadn't. Luckily, the traffic in Chicago is terrible, so it gave us time to prepare our whole presentation.

It was a great meeting, and the distributor agreed to sell invisibobbles through its network of 100,000 hair salons. Woohoo!!! It felt like we had started to crack America. (OK, not all 100,000 salons would necessarily buy invisibobble, but we had nonetheless started to crack America.)

There was still more to do in the US, however. As I said, it's home to some of the largest retailers in the world, bigger than anything we have in Europe. I'm a retail nerd, and I loved seeing the difference between European and American stores.

On another trip to the States, I decided I wanted to check out one of the world's largest grocery chains just to understand how life goes for many Americans and to see if it was the kind of place we wanted to stock invisibobble. This retailer was on the outskirts of a Texan town, and driving into the parking lot I could see that the online pickup area alone was the size of your average European supermarket. The store had a separate entrance for the food area and another for home and pharmacy. It had a garden centre and a place where you could have your car tires changed. Oh, and a Burger King was also integrated into the store.

Obviously, everything inside was HUGE. Far, far larger than in Europe. Potato chips took up both sides of one entire aisle. There were large bags of Cheetos Crunchy XXTRA Flamin' Hot, Cheetos Puffs Flamin' Hot, Cheetos Flamin' Hot Chipotle Ranch, Cheetos Flamin' Hot Lime and Cheetos Flamin' Hot Crunchy. Hell, there were even Cheetos and Doritos mixed in a bag.

Most of the shoppers were loading up huge trolleys with food and clothes, and the aisles seemed as long as football pitches. One large woman in a motorized cart was loading beer into the basket in front of her, while chewing her way through a whole loaf of bread she had picked off the shelf.

While we wanted to do well in America, we had to think about the kinds of stores we wanted to sell in. This one instinctively felt a bit too mass-market, and I wasn't sure it was right for us, especially since the upmarket stores turned out to be picky about where else our products were sold.

There was another large retailer in the US that I definitely thought we should get listed at: this time a pharmacy chain that we had already had some interest from. They had agreed to do a test run, putting invisibobbles in those giant bins that you see close to the checkouts in the hope that you'll spend just a few more bucks there.

That was OK, but we obviously also wanted to get listed with the rest of the hair accessories in the main part of the store.

The pharmacy chain's head office looked like a huge multi-storey car park with windows and inside there was row upon row of cubicles that looked like something out of a Dilbert cartoon. Each employee had their own cubicle, surrounded by fabric-covered boards that they clearly hadn't been allowed to customize with photographs or documents and they were all a uniformly dull brown shade. Around the edges of the room there were offices where some of the important people sat. These were windowless enclosures made up of three plain sides and one glass wall that overlooked the sea of cubicles. The even more important people had offices that actually had windows, but they were tinted and frosted to block out the sun. A bit like in Vegas, I never really knew what time of day it was in that building, because I couldn't really see outside.

I pitched invisibobble to the hair accessories buyer, a middle-aged woman who sat opposite me in one of the more important rooms, with a Dunkin' Donuts 24-ounce iced tea on her desk (that's almost the size of a bottle of wine). As I talked, she stared back at me with a blank expression, chugging at the iced tea through a straw every now and then.

Most of the time I received positive feedback as a young founder of a brand. Retail buyers rarely meet the actual founders of a company because so many brands don't have them. The brands are conceived of by new product development teams and marketing teams, which pass them on to sales teams to sell. Added to this, founders often leave the companies they started, because they quickly identify exit strategies, meaning they cash in and move on.

So, as I usually do, I enthusiastically poured my heart out to the 24-ounce iced tea woman, talking about how I started invisibobble because I got headaches, and how women love it because it doesn't leave a mark, and how well we were selling in Europe, and how cute our itsy bitsy packaging is, and how much I love the brand, and ...

"Honey, it's very cute that you're so excited," she interrupted. "But telling me a success story from Germany or the UK doesn't help me. This is America. It's a different world here. We sell a whole variety of products, and you need to stand out in the mix. The price you want me to pay is too high. The retail selling price is too much. Your products are too small. People won't understand why they are so expensive, and our customers will never buy them unless it's on impulse."

The woman also told me that because she had certain profit targets, she couldn't stock invisibobble because it would bring down the average margin for hair accessories. How would she be able to justify that? It was very frustrating.

And with that, she stood up, picked up her iced tea in one hand and extended the other to shake mine, and then I was through the door and back out into Dilbert-land.

It was a massive slap in the face.

But we had another chance. We had a meeting set up with the impulse-buy bins guy, the man in charge of convincing shoppers to grab something extra on their way out of the store. He was going to tell me how our test run had done.

He was a bald guy with another giant iced drink on his desk.

"I'm sorry, honey, but the sales aren't great. If you carry on like this, we're going to have to de-list you. You're very low down the ranking."

*Ouch.*

I took a deep breath. "Can you give me an idea of where we are in the ranking?" I asked.

The impulse-buy bins guy had an office, but it was the kind that had three solid walls and a view of the cubicles, and it was a lot smaller than the woman's. His desk was pretty narrow, and as he started pulling up our sales data on his computer, I could see it side-on.

I edged forward and peered at the screen for a second, and I could see that invisibobble was listed THIRD on his ranking. Third. It was just behind some poo smell-prevention drops you put in the toilet before you go, and they are meant to stop your bathroom stinking.

"But we're just after the poo drops!" I yelled.

"I didn't give you permission to look at my screen. That is confidential information," the bald guy yelled back, putting his giant cup down on the desk and turning the screen away.

I took a breath. "I'm sorry. But please could you extend the test to other stores for a few months?"

He eventually saw the funny side of my cheekiness and agreed, and we kept our bin listing. A few months later, we got a call back from the woman buyer at the retailer with the important office saying she wanted to place an order. We're now sold in all of their thousands of stores in the US, and it was our biggest deal yet.

# 21.
# The Icing
# on the Cake

**WHAT I LEARNED:**

- **However much success we had in one place, there would be a shit show in another**
- **Turns out, spiral-shaped hair ties can be patented**
- **Never underestimate the stress of having your own business**

It was great that we had the listing at the mass-market pharmacy chain in America but, as I mentioned before, the problem for many brands is that if you also want to sell in high-end stores, they won't take your product if you are selling it at a lower-end place.

One of these higher-end American retailers was very particular about what we could and couldn't do. They stock luxury brands permanently and then have smaller, hipper brands that they only list for a maximum of three years. It's a strategy that works very well for them, because the newness keeps people excited and coming back for more.

After we got the listing at the large, mass-market pharmacy chain, we needed to let the higher-end retailer know. So, a couple of weeks before the launch at the pharmacy, we dropped them an email just letting them know. Almost straightaway, I got the following email back:

> From: High-End Store Buyer
> To: Me
> Sent: Wed, 7 December 2016, 2.15 PM
> Subject: Re: Listing update
>
> **OK. We will immediately be de-listing all
> invisibobbles from all stores.**
>
> **Please send a return address for the goods.**
>
> **Regards.**

*Shit.*

We hadn't anticipated this response, and I got straight on the phone. Could we do a special line just for her? Would she consider that?

"The point is, Sophie, we don't list any brand that also exists in mass-market stores. It's not our strategy," she said, and that was it.

We scoured their website to find something, anything they sold that could also be found in mass stores.

Hair straighteners! There was a brand of hair straighteners on their website that you could also buy elsewhere, and they were the exact same brand name and type. I called her back.

"No, that's not correct. This isn't how we do things here," she said.

"But I can see the exact same hair straighteners, here on this other website," I protested.

"Well, if that's the case I'll get those hair straighteners de-listed from our stores immediately," she said, and hung up.

She was pretty angry, but at least we had tried. We decided that we'd had a good run with the high-end retailer, and now it was time to focus on mass-marketing. Getting a listing at the pharmacy chain would hopefully open the door for us at other stores.

A month or so later, we were astonished to get another email order from the high-end retailer. There must have been a mistake. I called the buyer again.

"I wanted to check. We got this order, but I'm guessing we shouldn't fulfil it because you're de-listing us," I said.

"No. Please fulfil it. And can we have a meeting? Bring your new concept," she said.

*Yes! And ohmygodweonlyhavetwoweekstopresentournewidea!*

Oh my god, we only had a couple of weeks to come up with a new idea. Up until then, our new product development had consisted of new colours for the original invisibobble and we hadn't changed anything about its size or shape. What could we do that would work for the high-end retailer that was genuinely different to our other products?

The one good thing that came out of all the disasters we had was something all growing brands have to think about: innovation. For the first three years or so of invisibobble's existence, we had relied on the fact that our product was new, people understood it and loved it, and that their understanding continued when we got better distribution and launched in new markets.

We had also done a great job of creating special collections a few times a year. They are limited-edition, and in summer 2015 we made one of my favourites, a savannah theme that we called Wild Whisper. We had a creamy-coloured hair tie with a lion on the box that we called Queen of the Jungle, a coral one called

Fancy Flamingo, a green one that Lisa loved called C U Later Alligator, and a pale blue one called Fata Morgana (it's a kind of heat haze).

Another collection I loved was one called Cookie Dough Craving, where we managed to infuse our invisibobbles with the sweet smell of baked cookies. We took over a cookie packaging production line for a day, so even the packs were authentic.

We know that when people browse the hair accessories section of a shop, they usually spend very little time there – about three seconds, to be exact. So, we have three seconds to convince someone to pick up our hair ties over either the retailer's own label version or even an elastic hair tie, which is why it's so important invisibobble looks different. I always wanted our packaging to be cute like candy, because candy is often multicoloured and looks tempting and is often an impulse buy.

But as much as the special collections tended to sell well, we knew we needed to innovate more. We were getting feedback from hairdressers and people on social media that they wanted a thicker hair tie that would stay fixed in their hair during exercise, and also that they wanted smaller ones that would be delicate enough to tie the end of a plait together. So we created the Power and the Nano in 2016 and launched them as the big and small sisters of the invisibobble Original. Obviously, you have to make it clear to people what they're for, so invisibobble Power is described as "The strong grip hair ring," and has two little diagrams on the packaging to show someone with thicker hair and another with a sporty look.

We also had to create something special for our high-end US retailer, and we had very little time to do it. The product needed to be different and somehow more luxurious than our Original, and so we came up with the idea for the Slim, which would look more delicate than the Original and would be a bit cooler. The material is of a slightly slimmer diameter than the Original and there are more coils, and we put together a presentation we sent to the buyer via email.

To make the Slim extra special, we also proposed making it in metallic colours – Bronze Me Pretty, Stay Gold and a silver we called Chrome Sweet Chrome – and the idea was that the hair tie looked more like a piece of jewellery someone would want to wear on their wrist.

A few weeks later, all of the existing Originals we were selling got returned to us, but then another email came through.

The buyer wanted to order $100,000 (about £78,000) worth of invisibobble Slim, which was huge. We estimated that would sell out in about two to three months, but after only six weeks, another order came through. The Slim had worked.

As with so much of the story of invisibobble (and most start-ups), we'd receive good news on the one hand, and then something bad would happen on the other. The 2016 invisibobble shit show included an event that none of us could have foreseen.

Somebody in the US had managed to patent the spiral hair tie shape.

Despite previously being told by various legal people that you can't patent a shape that is already in common use (coiled telephone cords, for example), it turns out some guy had found a way to do so. After all of our hard-won listings in beauty retailers across the US, toward the end of 2016 we started getting cease and desist letters. He'd done it years after we founded invisibobble and was being purely opportunistic, trying to find products to patent so he could then sue the companies that made the originals.

As I've said before, stores won't sell your products if there is any kind of legal issue, and this dude had been contacting our retailers, saying that he had the patent and our product was essentially breaching that. So, retailers started taking invisibobbles off their shelves. Every day for about a week, I'd get an email that would go something like this:

From: Central Legal Team
To: Me
Sent: Sat, 10 December 2016, 2.15 PM
Subject: Notification Of Item Suspension

**This is an auto-generated notification that the following goods will be returned to the seller.**

**Invisibobble Original True Black**
**Invisibobble Original Crystal Clear**
**Invisibobble Original Pretzel Brown**
**Invisibobble Original To Be Or Nude To Be**
**Invisibobble Original Blush Hour**
**Invisibobble Original Mint To Be**

**Invisibobble Power True Black**
**Invisibobble Power Crystal Clear**
**Invisibobble Power Pretzel Brown**
**Invisibobble Power To Be Or Nude To Be**

**Do not reply to this email.**
**The mailbox is unmonitored.**

To cut a long story short, we got into a massive fight with the guy, which got worse as Christmas approached. For about three weeks I'd wake up to several of these horrible, auto-generated emails from retailers across America. Sometimes we knew they were coming because our contacts had called us, and other times they were out of the blue. The guy systematically got his lawyers to send these nightmare letters to our hard-won retailers, who would then immediately contact us, saying they were withdrawing our product. It was as if someone was pressing a red alert button that was blaring out a message on loudspeaker that would send stores into a panic.

And because of the time difference, I'd stay up talking to retailers on the phone, sometimes late into the night, attempting to get them to keep invisibobble on their shelves for at least a week while we tried to sort out the legal mess.

I'd be on the phone to one retailer, while another email would come through, and then a second call would come on the line from the guy's lawyers and I'd have to switch over. And with each call I'd get angrier. This guy had me pushed up against a wall by the scruff of my neck and was demanding money; otherwise, his legal letters to the retailers would get ever more threatening.

By the time we closed the office at the end of the year, it still wasn't resolved. I'd flown back to Switzerland to spend time with my family. Hope had gone home to the UK, and Felix, Dani and Niki were somewhere on a German mountain. But it wasn't something we could leave dragging on until the new year. We needed to sort it out fast; otherwise, we would be faced with empty shelves across every retailer in the US.

Emails, texts and phone calls flew between me, the boys, the retailers and the guy's lawyers for days on end. He had abused a legal loophole, and I was damned if I was going to give him any money. But, after having our lawyers try everything to get him off our backs, I realized we were going to have to pay him off. Instead of enjoying dinner with my family on Christmas Eve, I was on the phone to his lawyers in the US until 11 at night. "We'll get back to you tomorrow," one of his legal team members said. I hung up. They were trying to make this as disruptive and painful as they could. *Tomorrow meant Christmas day! How dare they?*

Christmas morning came and went, and because of the eight-hour time difference my phone didn't ring until well after lunch. They finally accepted the offer. We had managed to pay the guy to go away back to his pest hole and never return, so we could focus on the good stuff: building our brand. I celebrated with a vodka and tonic, but it was definitely one of the worst times I'd had running this business.

———

To look at an invisibobble, you'd never know how much love and passion goes into creating those tiny, cute hair ties. I have friends with regular jobs say to me they're fed up with wherever they work and are envious of me for being my own boss, they want to take holidays any time they like, arrive when they want and take days off without notice, just living the good life. So many people say this to me, and I don't think anyone really understands *exactly* what it takes to start your own company and be successful at it.

Sometimes it's as if people think having your own business is a bit like making a cake: you decide what kind of creation you want to make, find the best ingredients and mix them carefully before baking. Then you sit back and do nothing while it rises in the oven, before decorating it beautifully and handing out slices for people to enjoy. You make a tidy profit in doing so; the icing on the cake! And then, surprise! The cakes carry on baking themselves and you just have to watch the money roll in for the rest of your days.

The reality is something like this:

Step 1: Decide you want to bake a new type of cake
Step 2: Try to ignore the fact that other people think it's a terrible idea and your new cake sounds disgusting
Step 3: Go ahead anyway, sourcing cake ingredients
Step 4: Receive ingredients, none of which you asked for, six weeks later

Step 5:    Cook in second-rate oven, using recipe in a foreign language

Step 6:    Watch cake bake until 1am while trying to avoid reaching the peak of the anxiety curve

Step 7:    Before cake is ready, try to sell slices of it to the people in step 2 by telling them how great it's going to be. They make faces at you because they're still not convinced

Step 8:    Get up at 4am to remove cake from oven and cool on wire rack. It's wonky, a strange colour and smells funny, but it's got potential

Step 9:    Repeat from step 3 onward until cake comes out perfectly

And that's a simplified version. I could also add:

Step 10:   Your oven explodes, destroying your kitchen. Spend weeks sourcing a new one. Lose tens of thousands

Step 11:   Realize that several other people have copied your cake idea. Spend a lot of time and money trying to destroy their recipes

Step 12:   Take ingredients supplier to court for ripping you off. Lose millions

Step 13:   People start enjoying slices of your cake. But they moan all the time: they want to pay much less for it, plus they want their own flavours, and they don't want you to sell it to other people. They really want to have their cake and eat it

Step 14:   Spend the rest of your life perfecting the recipe, finding the ideal oven, maintaining relationships with cake-sellers, thinking up new flavours, getting the baking time exactly right, testing out new decorations and checking that no one is copying your cakes. Most of all, make sure that your cakes are baked, decorated, sold and eaten with as much love as they always have been, right from day one. Repeat ad nauseam.

Don't get me wrong. I love invisibobble, and I love having my own business. But if you want to do your own thing, you have to get real. It's really not like baking a cake. It's like having your own children, who you ALWAYS have to put first. This is especially the case in the early years, when you need to love and nurture the business and products while they get off the ground. It's great fun, but it also includes butt fuck trips to the middle of nowhere, where you have to eat strange worm food and you're either getting up at 4am or going to sleep at 4am just to keep the business going by a thread.

The jetlag takes its toll on your body, and being away all the time affects your relationships. Having your own business means that partners, family and friends all become second priority. And for me that's OK, because invisibobble gives me meaning in life and motivates me to keep going. This is why we are all here. And yes, there are good times, but probably 80% is actually dealing with bullshit and yet more bullshit.

It takes a massive amount of love and dedication to get through the disputes, the fires, the fake factories and all of the D.O.D.s we have endlessly had to deal with. And that Christmas with the patent guy was definitely one of those times the invisible anxiety curve reached its peak, and I scraped by at the top of it for a while before finally coming back down.

# 22.
# From Craft Class Collage Kids to Grown-Up Innovators

80 MILLION INVISIBOBBLES SOLD

**WHAT I LEARNED:**

- **Not having an exit strategy means you can think long term about what's best for your brand**
- **Six years is way too long without bringing out a new product**
- **We found an innovative way of packaging our Waver hair clip**

In 2016, Felix and I got listed in *Forbes'* '30 Under 30 Retail and Ecommerce' list for Europe. *Forbes* is a well-respected American business magazine, and each year it produces various lists, creating rankings of everything from the world's wealthiest people to the most valuable soccer teams around the globe. Its reporters scour a long list of nominations and consult experts for the '30 under 30' Europe list, which is a collection of young people bringing new ideas to the continent. Being on this list is highly prestigious and it meant we got to attend exclusive events and meet other young entrepreneurs, as well as raise the profile of invisibobble.

But when we met other founders on the list, the conversations were often very similar.

"So, where did you raise money from?"

"We're self-funded," Felix or I would say.

"How come?"

"Well, we worked as ski instructors for a couple of seasons and saved $4,000 between us, which we spent on production."

"So how did you grow the business?"

"We were profitable from the start, and we've just reinvested those profits."

"What's your exit strategy?"

"We don't have one."

"Oh."

A lot of founders, especially in tech start-ups, are obsessed with the amount of investment they've had, plus who has provided that money. But if you take on investment, it means giving a chunk of your equity away, and you are answerable to the investor to a certain extent. That might work for businesses where they need expertise from the investor, but we've always preferred to do things ourselves and learn the hard way.

Entrepreneurs are also often focused on exit strategies – which means they've worked out when they want to sell their business. They either want to sell for a big chunk of money and move on to start the next thing, or they do a deal with whoever is investing or buying the company to stay on as a CEO for a certain amount of time and then, assuming all has gone well, cash in and move on.

If you have an exit strategy looming over you, it also means your goal is to make your business as valuable as possible.

That has an impact on marketing, for example, because you might be tempted to spend a lot on massive promotions or discounts, which might generate sales in the short term but aren't great for long-term brand health or profitability. Or you might launch new products quickly to show possible buyers that you have a large range of goods.

As we don't plan to sell invisibobble, it means we can think much longer term, rather than just making decisions based purely on how much cash they might generate in the short term.

In 2016, we had sold a total of 36 million invisibobbles. We were selling in 70 countries worldwide and through a few retailers and thousands of stores in the United States, and this was just based on our spiral hair ties. We were doing pretty well and being on the *Forbes* list was an amazing accolade, but just because we'd achieved good sales and press coverage didn't mean we couldn't push further. At that point, we hadn't invented any brand-new products, and we were pretty lucky to have got that far without doing so.

We didn't properly get organized as a business until really late – around the middle of 2016 – when we hired an interim Chief Financial Officer to help us with growth forecasts and budgeting. Up until then, I think we'd operated a bit like kids creating a random collage in an arts and crafts class, sticking a bit of sparkle here, gluing a piece of pretty material there, then looking at it from a distance and saying, "Oh that looks quite nice." We'd had an outside accountancy firm help us with our books, and we knew we were profitable, but there comes a point when you have to start basing decisions on facts and figures.

We needed to move from children's collage to art student's degree show (I don't think we're anywhere close to being in a fine art gallery – yet).

It finally felt like we were grown-ups running a business when we moved into a new, much larger office in 2017. We had massively outgrown the first place above the nightclub, so much so we had people sitting at temporary desks down the corridor, as well as Niki's farting French bulldog running around the office. We needed a bigger place where the dog at least could have a bit more room, and the fart smell would become more diluted. We moved into two floors of a new office building, still in Munich, and we separated the teams into marketing, research and development, finance and HR. The New Flag and invisibobble partners, Felix, Dani, Niki and I, could all sit in one large room together and are really focused on our invisibobble ambition: to be the world's go-to hair accessories brand.

Around this time, I also started thinking about my own role. I was the cofounder of invisibobble, but was I also the CEO?

I typed into Google:

"What does a CEO do?"

Google's answer was:
*A chief executive officer (CEO) is the highest-ranking executive in a company, whose primary responsibilities include making major corporate decisions, managing the overall operations and resources of a company, acting as the main point of communication between the board of directors (the board) and corporate operations and being the public face of the company.*

Hmm. That wasn't really what I did for invisibobble, and neither was it what I wanted to do. I'm good at making decisions, but I really don't like managing operations. I love to think big, create more ideas, continue to tell the story of invisibobble. But on a traditional corporate organization chart, a founder doesn't really sit anywhere. A founder can quite easily float, which means that many companies operate without one.

But when you operate without a founder and only have a CEO, you can lose that spark, that magic, the essence of a company or product that makes it special.

So then I Googled: "What does a founder do?"

The answers ranged from:
*A founder originally meant a person who forges steel; similarly, the founder of a company is forging the new entity.*

To:
*The primary role of a founder is that of an artist.*

I guess my role is somewhere in between, and I feel that my biggest responsibility is the wellbeing of invisibobble as a brand. It's really almost as if I treat it like a real person. It's not just does it have food and water, it's also does it feel happy? Where is it today and where does it want to go? What should it be associated with? I think about how consumers see invisibobble versus how we do as a business, and I want to get colleagues on board to believe in the same things I do. If you can do that, then you can take people with you, and they will be motivated to work in the brand's best interest. Products and structures are real, but a brand is more of a feeling that's hard to define. You can't touch it or see it, but you can believe in it. And if you don't believe in it, it doesn't exist.

If you want to establish yourself as a hair accessories brand, you need more than one type of product. So, in 2017, we started work on our first proper new product, which for a new business trying to grow was massively late, and we had been lucky that some enormous company hadn't come in and tried to dominate the hair tie category. After our visit to the metal bobby pin factory in China and seeing just how mass-produced they were, I thought it would be really cool if we could innovate a hair clip in some way, because it's something no one has really tried to do before.

We needed to apply the same principles to our hair clip as to invisibobble hair ties, which are that they don't leave a mark in your hair or give you a headache. Our hair clip would be hair-loving, in other words.

It started to become clear that we needed to work with one single piece of plastic, because it would be less likely to get caught, and it wouldn't go out of shape like metal bobby pins do. We had hired an in-house designer to help us, and I worked with him, as well as the research and development and marketing teams, to explain the kind of thing we thought would work.

Developing our hair clip, the Waver, was a lot about gut feeling – much more so than it was about numbers. If you Google 'hair clips,' you'll see that most of them have one of four or five types of metal base with different decorations, or they are the plastic claw-style clips that grip the hair. There are virtually no transparent hair clips around.

Trying to explain all of this to a male product designer with short hair was fairly amusing and involved a lot of demonstrations by me. It was a bit like when I first put the phone cord in my hair way back in December 2011, and practised various headbanging, swaying and waggling movements, except with metal hair slides. I'd click one into my hair with an 'ouch' (some of those clips are pretty brutal) and then get the designer to try to take it out of my hair and put it in someone else's.

For days, several women in the office would wear multiple metal clips to test how they left marks in their hair, and some of the men would too. Our office kind of turned into a hair clip museum for a moment there.

As well as employing an in-house designer, we also have lots of equipment in our new product development department. There's a virtual reality set we can use to understand how the Waver and other new products would work in someone's hair, an arts and crafts area where we create mock-ups, and a 3D printer to create prototypes.

Regular hair clips keep the hair in place by putting pressure between the two sides of the clip, so we knew that wouldn't work for ours. To make sure our new hair clip wouldn't leave a mark in people's hair, we knew it would probably need to be quite similar to our hair ties, in that pressure was evenly distributed on the hair. What we created, the Waver, has one side that is a kind of 3D helix spiral shape that you see in diagrams of DNA, which means it sits firmly in the hair without leaving a mark. The other side is curved, so it adapts to the shape of the person's head, and the end of the top part of the Waver hooks over the bottom part to close it. There are no hinges, and no metal. It's smooth all over because it's made from one piece of plastic, and that also means it can be created from a mould, can be made entirely by a machine, and doesn't need hand-finishing. Because of that, it's cost-effective for us to make the Waver in Europe.

Because they are made in Europe, we also needed to find somewhere that could pack them in a cost-effective way – and that packing had to happen by hand.

We looked into various options that would pay people a fair wage but would also be cost-effective, and the combination of both of those things is quite hard to find. Then we discovered prison labour. In most parts of Germany, prisoners are expected to work, and they get paid for doing so. Different prisons offer different levels of work, and packing Wavers fitted in with several around the country. Inmates can get promoted, and they can spend what they earn on small things like cigarettes or coffee, and the work is usually part of an initiative to reintegrate prisoners back into society toward their release. I believe there are complex reasons why someone ends up in prison and it's proven that when people work while they're behind bars, they reintegrate better into communities when they're released.

It's not always easy working with prisons, however, and it's something we considered carefully. On one visit I realized one of the inmates was from Peru, and I started speaking Spanish to him, but was quickly moved on by a guard. I learned that it's best to let production lines work without disturbing them. The Waver was the biggest innovation we'd made since the invisibobble Original hair tie and it took us 18 months from coming up with the idea to it being produced. Having an in-house design team is unusual in our industry, but for us it makes sense because it means we can work quickly. We create new products much more quickly now, but as the Waver was our first brand-new invention since our spiral hair rings, it took a while to get it right. Naming it was pretty easy because it looks wavy.

Our internal sales team only forecasted that we'd sell around 20,000 packets of three Wavers in the first three months, which is very little given that we sell our products in 80,000 stores around the world. Nevertheless, we took a chance and ordered about 300,000 packs, which would usually take around three months to sell in store.

All 300,000 packs sold out in two weeks. People loved it for all the reasons we hoped they would: it looked so different from any other hair clip, it was easy to use, and it didn't damage their hair.

Selling out so fast was fantastic, but it meant we were out of stock before we had even started a new production run, and it took months until we had more Wavers to send to stores. But then there came another problem. People started to complain that the Wavers were breaking.

We got notifications on social media and emails to our head office and people were returning them to stores, meaning our retailers were also getting in touch with us. We realized there was a problem with the end of the Waver when people were closing the two sides together.

Even though the polycarbonate we used is incredibly strong, it became weaker when we made it into the Waver shape. We were able to fix the problem in a few weeks by slightly changing the material, but we did lose sales because of it. Whenever we saw someone mention their broken Waver in a YouTube or Facebook comment, we would write back to them that we were excited about our new product launch and that we realized there was a problem, but that it had been fixed. It's not as if we're the only company ever to have launched a product that wasn't 100% right, but I hope that because we've now fixed it, people will forgive us and move on.

We could have avoided this if we'd done a test run in one or two countries to see how it sold, and if it did well, we could go ahead and order a ton. But we always said we wanted to make a big impact all over the world with our first innovation, and we believed that because people already knew invisibobble hair ties, they would recognize the brand and be ready for our new product. People were ready for the Waver, but it took us a second go to get it right.

# 23.
# Invis-a-booble.
# Imboba-vizzle.
# Invibi-sobble.

**WHAT I LEARNED:**

- **Think very carefully before you take on anyone bigger than you**
- **If people are confused by your brand name, you can turn that into a positive thing**
- **I've always hated anything that's dull or 'vanilla'**

We learned some legal lessons the hard way. The Very Hard Way. As soon as we discovered that the spiral shape of our hair ties could actually be patented, we then patented the shape of some of our products in certain parts of the world. One example is our small hair Nano hair tie.

But one Friday night, I was casually browsing the aisles of one of my favourite German supermarkets (as you do), when I noticed some cute little cube boxes piled up in one of those large bins near the checkout. I got closer and then saw to my horror that it was an exact replica of the invisibobble Nano. It was a product we had patented. For once, we were on the front foot, and we could DESTROY whoever had done this to us.

On Monday morning, I asked our legal person (we hired an in-house legal assistant as soon as the copies started getting out of hand a couple years before) to draft the supermarket chain a cease and desist letter, explaining that they were selling direct copies of OUR products, and that they would have to be removed from the shelves.

The supermarket doesn't have a central distribution hub, so the company would have to go to collect the fake Nanos from every single shop that was selling them, which would be a massive job. And this store has thousands of shops. *Yes! Take that, sucker!*

The letter worked, and the products were removed, but I got too cocky. What I didn't know at the time was that the person who had copied invisibobble came from a HUGE corporation and would therefore have a lot of money to throw at lawyers.

About a week after we had sent our cease and desist letter to the supermarket, we were contacted by one of the high-end German retailers that sold invisibobble, saying they had received a cease and desist letter to stop selling our products. And, of course, the letter came from the fake Nano guy's company.

We discovered that he had given our invisibobble packaging to a legal team to see if everything we stated on the packaging was legally compliant, and there was one thing they had found that he could use against us. "Eco-friendly colours," used to be one of our product claims and we put it there because Mei (remember her?) had promised us the colours were eco-friendly. We asked her a thousand times for a certificate from the factory to prove this but, as with so many other things, she never gave us one. The fake Nano guy was claiming unfair competition because he said we were falsely stating that our colours were eco-friendly.

Our naivety in business had sometimes helped us – because we didn't know the 'rules,' we had license to do things in our own way – but this time our lack of knowledge bit us hard. Many of our European retailers started getting in contact, having received similar letters, and suddenly all of our products were yet again being removed from the shelves – this time in Europe. And you have a very limited time to sort this out. If you don't, retailers will just shut down and say they won't deal with you in the future.

One of our mass-market German retailers was super helpful and understanding, but one of the higher-end pharmacy chains took us off their shelves for about two months.

It was another horrible, worrying time for me. Every time something like this happened, I would start back up the anxiety curve and hover at the top of it until things looked like they were getting sorted out. It's not just the brand I worry about, it's all the people we had working for us by then and the overheads we were paying in rent. Being a small brand in a small company in a big, bad business world is hard.

What we learned from the experience with the fake Nano guy is not to start picking on someone else without making sure you are absolutely bulletproof yourself. Of course he had to bear the cost of taking his stock out of all the German supermarkets, but what he did to us was proportionally a lot worse. In the end, we had to sign an agreement to let him carry on selling his products; otherwise, he was going to find other ways of coming to get us.

Now we have long documents that legally support all of our product claims and why we are different from other hair ties, but it took a long time (and a lot of money) to get it right. And unfortunately, some of my experiences in business have made me much less trusting of people. I expect them to have bad intentions, which isn't how I want to feel, but having been burned too many times I am now much more cautious.

Entrepreneurship is sometimes talked about as if it's some kind of fairy tale, but it really isn't. You go through a lot of crap, and you just have to keep pushing through it and never give up. It's not like you start a company and then chill. You start a company and work your butt off. You don't take holidays or, if you do, you sometimes have to cancel them to work, because in the beginning especially, you are the only workforce there is. A lot of founders can barely afford to live, certainly to start with, because EVERYTHING goes into their business.

By the end of 2017, invisibobbles were sold in 50,000 locations around the world, so we were doing pretty well. And sure, we could have stopped there. But we have a saying in the business. We talk about 'constructive dissatisfaction,' which means that, however much we do, we are not satisfied in the long term, because the next big win, the next product development, might be just around the corner. Even if we sign a deal with a retailer that's worth half a million dollars, we're pushing for the next one. And that's why our dissatisfaction is constructive, because it helps us grow. We could have said, "Hey, we're done" when we were 22 and the business was doing pretty well but, as Niki says, complacency is the death of success. As soon as you pat yourself on the back for achieving something, there will be ten other people behind you trying to take that away.

Niki has a presentation slide that he always shows in company meetings, which is of the Olympic swimmer Michael Phelps standing on the blocks in the seconds before a race. He's completely focused on himself and conquering the pool he's about to jump into. The point is, we want to just focus on ourselves and not look left and right or look too much at what the competition is doing. Because if you do, you stumble. You can't be completely blinkered, and you can't ignore the market, but if you look at what everyone else is doing and try to do the same thing, you'll never win.

In my opinion, the people who copied our products were not winners. It's a bit like a smartphone. No one knew they needed one until they were created, but they are a huge success. In a similar way, everyone thought bobby pins or hair clips were fine the way they were until we showed them that there might be another, better opportunity.

Up until the end of 2017, we had relied on good PR to get our name and products known, and of course having the right distribution was absolutely crucial. We had never spent money on advertising invisibobble, but toward the end of 2017, I felt that we needed to make more of a mark in America. We had great distribution, but the concern was that retailers would start making their own-label version of our product, and we needed a way to make people understand that invisibobble is the original spiral hair tie (and the best, of course).

We hired an ad agency in New York, and I flew over to brief them with Lisa (I ended up flying to New York from Munich for only about 18 hours because the flight was so delayed). It was a good meeting, and I spent ages explaining how I founded invisibobble with Felix, how we'd reached a certain level of distribution in Europe and the US, and now we needed to make sure our consumers understood us. We started talking about the product benefits, but I wasn't keen for them to be a focal point of our advertising because people can still pick up own-label spiral hair ties when they're at the shelf in a store. Although other companies can – and have – copied our product, the one thing they can't copy is our name.

About a year into starting the business, we had realized that people were really not understanding the name 'invisibobble,' and we got to the point where we decided we were going to have to call it something else. We locked ourselves in a room for three days to brainstorm alternatives. But we didn't come up with anything else, so we stuck with it.

A common mistake is to name a brand after the unique selling point of one product. So 'invisibobble' represents the fact that our hair ties don't leave a mark – that's the invisible part of the name. But actually, that name could have limited us when launching other products, because technically a hair clip is not a hair bobble, for example.

At one point, we were thinking of using 'invisi' in front of other types of hair accessory, so for example the Waver could have been the 'invisiclip' But after discussing this at length, we decided that we would keep the invisibobble brand as the master brand, and then have our product names 'underneath,' like the Waver, Bunstar and Sprunchie, which is a scrunchie but with an invisibobble inside it. The technical term for this is 'brand architecture,' but of course we had no idea that concept existed when we started the business.

Experienced marketers in a large company would probably have developed the entire product range from day one, with a brand architecture in place. But I'm not so sure that would have worked for us. Because if we had presented the spiral hair tie, as well as a plastic hair clip plus a new type of scrunchie that had never been seen before to a retail buyer, they would have looked at the range and said no, all your products are really weird and way too different to other hair accessories. Thanks, but no thanks.

But anyway, right from the start, people have had trouble saying and remembering 'invisibobble' as a brand name. I'd even go so far as to say it's the single biggest problem we have had in terms of developing the brand. We knew that people remembered spiral hair ties as a product, but they were less good when it came to remembering invisibobble as a brand name, or appreciating that we make the original traceless hair ties.

Toward the end of our meeting with the ad agency, I touched on the name and explained that I didn't think that putting 'invisi' and 'bobble' together was a problem. I actually thought it was a great name, but apparently it's the single most complicated thing on earth.

A week or so later, the agency presented us with ideas for three different campaigns. I don't even remember the first two, but the third one made me laugh out loud. On the screen, they showed me one word:

Invis-a-booble.
Then another flicked onto the screen:
Imboba-vizzle.
And finally:
Invibi-sobble.

The whole campaign was based around the fact that no-one could pronounce 'invisibobble' correctly. The idea was to shoot it in the style of an over-the-top perfume ad, switching between three actresses holding a pack of invisibobbles and exclaiming "fashionable," "reliable," "desirable" in their best sexy fragrance voices. But when it came to saying "invisibobble," they just can't say it correctly, coming out with "invis-a-booble," "imboba-vizzle" or "invibi-sobble" instead. A director coaches the women on how to say "invisibobble," which they finally do, before the ad ends with a voiceover saying, "invisibobble. That simple." I loved the ad because it was all about the name, which is the single biggest problem we have with our brand, and it managed to communicate everything in a really amusing but simple way.

But some people hated it.

They hated it because they said it was sexist, or anti-feminist, because the director in the ad is a guy who is trying to explain to women how invisibobble should be pronounced. But the women definitely don't come across as stupid, plus the ad is a parody of a perfume commercial, and the point is that they can't figure out the name of the product.

People loved it because we'd been honest about people mis-saying the name and they were posting comments on Facebook, delighted by the fact that we were mocking perfume ads that take themselves way too seriously. And those that hated it for being 'anti-feminist'? They were so outraged they would tag ten other people on social media. Perfect.

Some brands are very vanilla when it comes to marketing, but that doesn't work for me. I loved the fact that the ad was polarizing because it meant people would talk about it. The good thing was that whether they loved it or hated it, they were telling their friends.

It's always hard to measure the exact impact of advertising on sales, but we knew the campaign was popular because you can measure the number of times people watched it or clicked on it. We put it on Facebook in June 2018, and it performed a lot higher than average for hair and beauty ads.

I've always had a hatred of anything vanilla, or bland, or things that are just 'fine.' I guess if I'm reflecting on myself, I have a fear of being vanilla. A very large goal for me in life, is that, if I think "How am I doing?" the big question I ask myself is: "Is what I'm doing average?" The biggest way I can let myself down is to be average, because if you're average, you just blend into the masses. And with something like vanilla ice cream, everybody likes it, but it's nobody's favourite. If you had a sushi-flavoured ice cream, you're definitely going to talk about it and remember it, because you'll either love it or hate it – although most probably the latter.

I think that's probably partly why I came up with the idea for a spiral hair tie in the first place, and loved it, because it just looked so weird. Definitely not vanilla.

# 24.
# Build That Wall, Haha

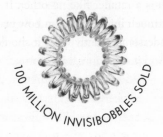

**WHAT I LEARNED:**

* **Brands have a love-hate relationship with Amazon**
* **An in-store wall costs a shedload of money, but it's worth it**
* **Apparently, 15mg of THC will get you hiiiiiiigh**

I haven't really talked about selling online much, because it hasn't been something we've done a lot of. In 2012, we started off with an online store we set up via Shopify, but closed it down after about a year because we started getting proper distribution into salons and retailers. It's not really financially viable for us to have our own online shop (for now), because the delivery charges we'd have to add would probably be about the same as a three-pack of invisibobbles.

And of course, there's one massive online retailer I haven't mentioned so far, which brands tend to have a love-hate relationship with.

Amazon.

As we're a brand that doesn't have its own shops, we rely on retailers to sell invisibobble on our behalf, and as I've explained, that means a LOT of negotiations and relationship building, sleepless nights, flying around the world and having to think creatively when a retailer predicts we'll have flat year-on-year sales.

And Amazon is a retailer like no other. It's very powerful, because it has so much information on how people shop, and it can therefore understand exactly what it should be selling and for how much. And it can apply this information to creating its own label brands, just like a brick-and-mortar retailer.

But it's also a place where competition is fierce. If you search on Amazon for GHD (one of the biggest hair straightener brands out there), for example, the top of the results page will show GHD straighteners as a sponsored listing, followed by another row of sponsored, non-GHD hair straighteners. Then the next row is all GHD products. Click on one, and you go to the product page. But just after the description of the straighteners, there's an ad for a different, but similar brand, at a cheaper price. So, at every step of the way, Amazon makes money by showing ads that may tempt people away from your brand.

And unless you very tightly control your distribution (Gap and Zara only sell in their own shops for example, but Adidas sells trainers in a variety of places), chances are you'll end up on Amazon anyway via resellers (also known as the 'grey market').

As with other retailers, if Amazon gets any kind of legal letter or any suggestion that there are copies of a product being sold online, they will immediately shut you down. Toward the end of 2018, another hair accessories company decided to find some old patent for a hair tie that looked vaguely like invisibobble. And that company wrote to Amazon and decided to tell them that we were in breach of this random patent, and so Amazon, in its wisdom, stopped selling invisibobble online.

It's very hard to speak to an actual human at Amazon, and they deal with most seller issues via an online system that can take ages. While I was trying to get them to start selling invisibobble again, I also wanted to get back at the rival hair accessories company. So, I did the unthinkable. I called one of the guys who we had had a fight with over a patent. I called and left messages several times, but he never rang me back. Eventually, I sent him an email.

From: Me
To: Patent Guy
Sent: Sat, 1 December 2018, 9.01 AM
Subject: Christmas Has Come Early

**Dear Patent Guy,**

**Remember me? It's Sophie from invisibobble. We got into a row about patents and I gave you a big present one Christmas day to go away.**

**Now that I've got your attention, I wanted to let you know that there's another hair tie company selling on Amazon and they've managed to shut us down because they claim there's some old patent hanging around that we're in breach of.**

**Can you do me a favour? Could you report XXXX company for being in breach of YOUR patent?**

**I'd love an early Christmas present.**

**Kindest regards,**

**Sophie.**

I never heard back from the Patent Guy, but let's just say all of a sudden the other hair accessories company wasn't on Amazon anymore. But then it got completely out of hand, because that rival hair accessories company then reported the Patent Guy's products, and at one point, there wasn't a single spiral-shaped hair tie available on Amazon, just in time for Christmas. It took a few weeks to sort out and it was not a very happy Amazon Christmas that year.

We got listed in a specialist beauty chain in the US, one that started as a salon supplier and now sells to regular customers. We got our listing there in 2018, and that was fine, but I wanted more.

I wanted a wall.

A wall is where we could have our own, dedicated chunk of display space in a store, that has our own, separate branding and colours, and very obviously only belongs to invisibobble. If you look at the regular hair tie section of a store, it will often say something like 'great value' at the top of it, because normal, unbranded or own label hair elastics are just cheap things stapled to a piece of cardboard 50 at a time. Having our own wall is a bit like the hair accessories equivalent of a branded high-end makeup stand in a store.

And because we essentially reinvented the hair accessory category with products that have a genuine point of difference (they don't leave a mark in your hair), with innovative packaging, I knew we could also create a wall display that looked completely different.

And this particular store chain is perfect for invisibobble, because it's full of young, hip women who love brands and love the shopping experience when they go to this beauty chain. They have about 1,200 outlets across the States and are seen as highly influential. They get a lot of press attention and their in-store associates are often hair and beauty junkies who care a lot about the products they sell.

But when you want to take up more room in a store, you have to negotiate hard. If you want more room for your brand, then products from other companies have to make way for yours and you have to pay the retailer for that privilege. Then, instead of simply shipping boxes of products to the store, you also have to ship the wall displays, with the products already mounted on them, and you have to wrap those up so carefully, so they don't get damaged and cost a ton of money. And because retailers treat walls like advertising space, you also have to pay to be there.

But despite the big investment we needed to make, for me, the wall was a MASSIVE deal, because it was the first time we could 'own' a part of a store. Every time I had a meeting with our sales team, I'd ask, "Where is our wall?" and sometimes I'd get a vague answer, like "Oh, they don't let hair accessories have walls." But we are all about pushing the boundaries, ignoring the rules and, let's face it, making things up as we go along. In my mind, "They won't let us" is just an excuse. For me, a wall in one of the most prestigious beauty retailers in the world was a huge deal, like the realization of my vision for invisibobble. It took us maybe a year of negotiations to get them to agree to our wall, and then another six months to get it designed, made and shipped to their stores.

The design was super important to me because it allowed us to communicate with consumers in-store properly for the first time. People don't have me in their ear telling them all about invisibobble, but we can use our packaging and what we put on our wall to show them how we're different. Our wall is about the size of half a door and we're able to tell a bit more of the brand story and values. The other great thing about a wall is that it's literally screwed to the … wall. Unlike cardboard stands, it can't easily be moved or removed – we are there permanently, bar someone crowbarring us away. The marketing term for that is to be 'sticky.'

After a year and a half of designing, researching, negotiating and paying out a ton of money, our walls were finally being delivered into stores. I was getting photos of them but hadn't seen them in the flesh. In June 2019, I headed out to Los Angeles to check out our wall for the very first time. I was there in the city for about a week having meetings and it was wasn't until the end of the trip that I got a chance to visit a store with Ignacio, one of the guys who had started working for invisibobble in America. Ignacio had already seen the wall and was pretty happy with it, but he insisted that we needed to go together, with champagne, to toast our new wall.

Thinking about seeing the wall for the first time, I didn't know whether I would laugh, cry or shrug. We'd agreed to visit the store on a Friday afternoon after all our meetings were done. On Wednesday, Ignacio and I were sitting at breakfast. He leaned across the table toward me.

"Dude. I bought something," he whispered.

"What, another pair of trainers?" (Ignacio is very into designer sneakers.)

"No," he said, his eyes darting left and right. "I went to Med Men."

"What's Med Men?!" I asked.

"The weed store! I bought edibles!"

"Huh?"

"Yes, dude, it's legal here."

He reached down and handed me a small, white box which claimed the contents were "made with real fruit and natural flavours." I opened it, and inside were some small, red, chewy gummies.

"We should totally eat these at some point!" Ignacio said.

"OK. Let's wait for the weekend, no?"

Friday afternoon came, and this being LA, we sat by the hotel pool on our laptops doing emails after a long morning of meetings.

I looked up, and there was the little white box on the table.

"We should take one now," Ignacio said, whispering. (Whispering even though it's perfectly legal to take cannabis recreationally in California.)

I picked up the box: 5mg THC per gummy, it stated.

"What does that even mean?" I said.

I Googled it, and THC is the psychoactive part of the marijuana plant, the part that gets you high. And the internet told me that the scale of THC dosing goes from zero to 100. Up to 2.5mg is considered micro-dosing, so you don't even really feel it.

Then it said that 5mg or 10mg or even 15mg are minimum doses for getting high (by the way, always seek expert advice if you're going to legally take THC – don't take my word for it). I'm thinking if you get to maybe 60mg, that's when you're the equivalent of 7 Jager bombs in, and 100mg is like the world is spinning and you're vomiting everywhere.

And like drinking a beer, it takes time for the active ingredients to take effect, maybe an hour. So, we both took one gummy, which just tasted like a chewy sweet, and carried on with our emails.

At some point I looked over to Ignacio and asked if he could feel any kind of effect. He couldn't.

Then another little white box appeared on the table. "These are stronger," he said. He took out a gummy, bit it, and gave half to me. And suddenly, I worked out we'd each consumed between 12mg and 15mg. It was time to get ready to go to the beauty store to finally see the wall I'd been dreaming about.

It started in the shower.

I was shampooing my hair, and suddenly, I could feel each hair follicle with my hands, and there were millions of them. I had far, far too much hair on my head. I managed to get showered and dressed, and as I was walking downstairs to meet Ignacio, I was screwing my toes up like claws and I could feel all ten of them, individually, in my shoes. And then as I was waiting for Ignacio, everything felt as if I was a character in a film, and suddenly all the people in the hotel were under water, we were in the ocean, and a storm was coming … Then Ignacio appeared.

"Hi, we have to go get the champagne," he said.

The difference between 5mg and 12mg of THC is apparently massive because I went from feeling zero difference to being as high as the hot LA sky in the half-hour I spent getting ready.

We went to a grocery shop, and holding on to a small bottle of champagne, some crisps and two plastic cups seemed to be the hardest thing I'd ever done. And in the cab on the way to the beauty chain, things got progressively worse. Because I'd eaten a gummy rather than smoked a joint, I got a prolonged high rather than a short hit. I was pressing my face up against the side of the Uber, feeling like everything was unreal, asking myself, *What am I doing? Oh yes, remember, Sophie, you're in an Uber, on the way to a beauty store to see your wall of invisibobbles, with your face there, right in the middle of the wall, with the invisibobble logo on it and everything, its own special section, and look down there! There is a champagne bottle rolling around on the floor of this Uber, and there is Ignacio, our American salesperson, and he's next to me in this car, which is an Uber, and why are we in an Uber again?*

Finally, we got to the store, which was surrounded by other stores and a huge car park. I could barely get out of the car. This moment, which I'd waited for and worked on for so long, was finally here, and I was so high I could barely move. The gummies seemed to have done nothing at all to Ignacio, who started walking toward the entrance. I started laughing. I was laughing so hard I didn't think I should be seen in public, but I really wanted to get into the store to see our wall. I grabbed Ignacio's hand, walking close enough behind him so that people couldn't see my face, but not close enough that I would tread on the backs of those designer sneakers.

We went in. Everyone started looking at us, especially me. They were staring at me, and with every step we took down the aisle, more and more eyes were on us. The aisle was long, so long that I couldn't see where it ended, and this made me laugh even harder. We kept walking, and the people kept staring. Finally, we got to the wall. Our invisibobble wall. There it was, but all I could do was laugh so hard I cried.

I managed to recover a little composure, and once I did, I started counting to make sure all the hooks were there, with invisibobble packs hanging off them. They call them pegs, and all 45 were present and correct. Four of the pegs are seasonal, so we can display our special collections on them, and the best thing about it is we get to choose exactly what we display and when. It looked great, and I think I would have been on a massive high when I saw it even if I hadn't eaten gummies laced with THC.

After our wall viewing, we were meant to go to dinner with a well-known LA PR guy, but I was so high I couldn't even speak. Ignacio went on his own, and I went back to the hotel to bed. At 5.30pm. It wasn't even dark, but I slept pretty well, apart from waking up every so often with the munchies, and I would crawl over to the mini bar to attack it. I'd eaten everything by 5.30am, so at that point I got up and headed out for a run around a weirdly empty Beverly Hills.

As I jogged back to the hotel, I smiled to myself. We'd got our wall.

# 25.

# The Good
# Old Days

**WHAT I LEARNED:**

* Maintaining a start-up culture is crucial when you grow —
  and you can do this by storytelling
* I'm taking a deep breath and getting 'out there' as a founder
* Bald guys know what invisibobble is

When I look back at what we've done with invisibobble, I'm pretty proud. Sure, we've made some mistakes, but for me that's the only way to learn.

It's eight years since I sat in my university dorm room for a week that cold December, trying to think of a product I could make and sell. At university, Felix and I wanted to use our time in a more meaningful way than just going out and drinking vodka tonics seven nights a week and occasionally spending the day studying. I don't think we would ever have imagined or dreamed that invisibobble would become what it has. In fact, Felix said there is "not a chance in hell" he would ever have imagined working in the hair accessories business when he was younger.

There's also no chance in hell our parents would have given us money to start a hair accessories company (or for any kind of company, for that matter). The combination of Felix's business acumen and my creative vision has helped us become successful, as well as total trust of our business partners Dani and Niki, and invisibobble is now fully part of New Flag, becoming one of its own brands. With that, I have also moved into New Flag to become the fourth CEO and shareholder, but of course remain the mother of invisibobble.

I realize that we were lucky to find great business partners and accept that being able to do things like go to university overseas is a privilege, but I think that masses of hard, hard work and dedication has made invisibobble a success. We could have given up when we were copied, when our shipment set on fire or after discovering our factory was fake, but we drove onward and upward.

In April 2019, we celebrated selling our 100 millionth invisibobble hair tie, but in some ways, I feel like we're just getting started.

My dream would be to open invisibobble flagship stores in New York and London, which would be beautiful and bright, the hair accessories equivalent of a high-end but accessible makeup outlet. The stores would have our full range of products, from the invisibobble Original in Crystal Clear to the Bowtique in lots of different colours and our new Wrapstar, an invisibobble combined with a long ribbon that launched in Germany in 2020.

At the store, there would be a free up-do bar and a customization station, where people could create their own three-packs that could be packaged with their names. A photobooth could take pictures and post directly to Instagram, and people would be able to enter a competition to win a silver or gold invisibobble bracelet. And of course, there would be a seasonal wall with all of our special collections and collaborations. It would be like a creative and colourful candy shop for your hair. Flagship stores like this are massively expensive because of the rent you have to pay, but what they lack in margins they make up for in brand love and recognition.

I would also like to sell directly via invisibobble.com, but this isn't cost-effective for us right now. It would be too expensive for us to fulfil orders if someone is only spending a small amount. And even though we are an innovative business that has created an entirely new category and pushed retailers to take a risk on us, we are actually pretty careful ourselves. We don't spend a lot on marketing, for example, and will always look for ways to be efficient (but not stingy) with money.

Speaking of marketing, we've evolved from the days of sneaking into fashion shows and hoping celebrities would pick up our invisibobbles, to carefully planning our Instagram feed and holding fun events for hairdressers. In summer 2019 I set up my own @sophie_invisibobble Instagram account, as we realized that people were interested in the story of invisibobble, and around that time I also started writing this book.

Being the cofounder of an eight-year-old business is about growing up with the brand. It's reflective of who we are as people. As we have matured, we've understood more about ourselves and how we want to run our company, and learned about how to have good relationships with each other and our customers.

I've gone from being quite coy about invisibobble (remember how I ran around the corner in the Swiss ski resort to cry when we got our first major UK listing, not wanting to tell anyone?) to becoming more of the face of the brand. Even though I was shy about being 'out there' to start with, I feel that giving a behind-the-scenes glimpse of life at invisibobble is something that people are interested in. Having a founder full stop is not something many brands still have, and so it makes sense for us to use that to our advantage. It's still weird seeing pictures of myself on our displays, or videos of me on YouTube, but I'm getting used to it.

We sometimes talk in the office about the 'good old days' when invisibobble was a super scrappy start-up, and Felix and

I would be opening boxes of hair ties from China, probably having to scrub them in the sink, and then spreading them all over the floor of Felix's parents' living room. And while we now have an organized business, I do miss the times when we had to do everything ourselves, like when I had to pretend to be from invisibobble's legal 'team,' or when we told a distributor we were pitching to that we were 22, even though we were still teenagers.

We work hard to keep that culture going by having monthly catch-ups with the whole company at our in-house bar. Over a vodka tonic (or a beer – my preferred drink these days since I live in Bavaria where beer is literally part of the traditional breakfast meal), I'll sometimes tell the story of how Felix and I had to pack a pallet with tens of thousands of invisibobbles – twice – and then got fined because we'd done it all wrong, or I'll talk about the time when we discovered our Chinese factory was just a front.

I've also told our team about my TEDx talk. In it, I focused on three things: that ideas for new products or businesses can be phenomenally successful (in my limited experience) if they are 1) simple, 2) cheap and 3) you don't have to be an expert in your chosen industry. Simplicity is a beautiful thing because it meant we could roll our product out fast – and if it hadn't worked, we would have failed quickly and cheaply. Not being experts in our chosen field (and this especially applies to Felix) wasn't a problem, because we didn't know the rules, and that meant we did things our own way – sometimes breaking the rules in the process.

What we did have was a vision, which was to brand a hair tie so that it is associated with a lifestyle and that meant we could sell invisibobbles in fashion outlets and department stores as well as regular drugstores. Not being insiders meant we didn't place artificial limits on ourselves, because we didn't know the rule that said hair ties were just cheap commodities stapled to pieces of cardboard and only sold in high-street chains.

And my final point about starting our business cheaply – well, as I've said, invisibobble started with the equivalent of 1,350 vodka tonics.

I try to explain that we're successful because we don't do things that everyone else has done, and that means we have taken risks. I want everyone in the company to understand the bigger picture of invisibobble, and that could mean someone who isn't in the new product development team pitches their idea to us, for example. It also means we give people license to try things and risk failure. But if it doesn't work, never mind – we move on. I'm much happier for someone to take a risk and it not work than analysing something 50 times and then not doing something because they weren't bold enough to do it.

Our company culture is also positively affected by the fact that we don't have an exit strategy. Many people in 'regular' jobs dream of becoming entrepreneurs, and as I am fortunate enough to be living that dream, why would I give that up?

Evan Spiegel, the founder of Snapchat, is often asked why he turned down a reported $3 billion offer from Facebook to buy his company.

"The best thing is that no matter whether or not you sell, you will learn something very valuable about yourself. If you sell, you will know immediately that it wasn't the right dream anyway. And if you don't sell, you're probably onto something. Maybe you have the beginning of something meaningful," was the reasoning Spiegel gave during a commencement address at the University of California's Marshall School of Business in 2015. For me, invisibobble is that 'something meaningful,' something I love and I want others to as well. I care very much what consumers think of our products, and I scour social media every day to read comments (good and bad), and I still respond to people directly. Recently I found myself spending 20 minutes DM-ing someone on Instagram to help her choose the right type of invisibobble.

I know that we're not changing the world with invisibobble; however, the reason I thought of the idea in the first place was because I needed to find a way to wear my hair up without getting headaches. We get messages every day from women who use invisibobble telling us how we have in fact 'changed their lives' because they now no longer get headaches. Seeing messages like this is really what gives us purpose. As I said, we are not changing the world, but we are changing a small aspect of millions of people's lives every day for the better. And for me, that's something worth living for.

And far from sitting back and letting the business run (though I can now take holidays without checking my phone every hour for the next disaster of the day), it takes more love and dedication than ever to keep invisibobble as what marketing people call the 'category king'; to keep pushing our brand on a global level. I travel about a third of the year, which sounds glamorous but mainly means I have intricate knowledge of the inside of airports, cramped planes and strange airline food.

To give an idea, here's everywhere I flew in 2019:

| | |
|---|---|
| 04.01 | Chicago - London |
| 05.01 | London - Madrid |
| 06.01 | Madrid - Munich |
| 12.02 | Munich - New York |
| 17.02 | New York - Montreal |
| 19.02 | Montreal - Minneapolis |
| 19.02 | Minneapolis - San Francisco |
| 22.02 | San Francisco - Munich |
| 04.03 | Munich - London |
| 05.03 | London - Munich |
| 01.04 | Munich - Tel Aviv |
| 04.04 | Tel Aviv - Munich |
| 25.04 | Munich - Madrid |
| 28.04 | Madrid - Munich |
| 10.05 | Munich - Copenhagen |
| 12.05 | Copenhagen - Munich |
| 17.05 | Munich - Lisbon |
| 19.05 | Lisbon - Munich |
| 07.06 | Munich - Berlin |
| 09.06 | Berlin - Munich |
| 11.06 | Munich - Los Angeles |
| 18.06 | Los Angeles - Boston |
| 19.06 | Boston - Munich |
| 21.06 | Munich - Copenhagen |
| 23.06 | Copenhagen - Munich |
| 12.07 | Munich - Budapest |
| 14.07 | Budapest - Munich |
| 19.07 | Munich - Barcelona |
| 21.07 | Barcelona - Munich |
| 24.07 | Munich - Paris |
| 25.07 | Paris - Munich |

| | |
|---|---|
| 01.08 | Munich - London |
| 01.08 | London - Munich |
| 04.09 | Munich - Mallorca |
| 08.09 | Mallorca - Munich |
| 09.09 | Munich - Paris |
| 10.09 | Paris - Munich |
| 17.09 | Munich - London |
| 17.09 | London - Munich |
| 27.09 | Munich - Los Angeles |
| 05.10 | Los Angeles - Munich |
| 14.10 | Munich - Amsterdam |
| 15.10 | Brussels - Munich |
| 15.10 | Munich - Johannesburg |
| 16.10 | Johannesburg - Cape Town |
| 17.10 | Cape Town - Johannesburg |
| 17.10 | Johannesburg - Munich |
| 04.11 | Munich - London |
| 10.11 | London - Munich |
| 14.11 | Munich - Manchester |
| 16.11 | Manchester - Munich |
| 19.11 | Munich - Frankfurt |
| 19.11 | Frankfurt - Shenzhen |
| 23.11 | Shenzhen - Beijing |
| 23.11 | Beijing - Munich |
| 29.11 | Munich - Madrid |
| 01.12 | Madrid - Berlin |
| 01.12 | Berlin - Munich |
| 09.12 | Munich - Paris |
| 09.12 | Paris - Munich |

That's 60 flights – and I don't see that number letting up any time soon.

I would love for invisibobble to become simply the name people use to refer to any spiral hair tie, like Hoover or Google or Kleenex, because the brands that achieve that status are really the pioneers in their categories. But those brands have a responsibility to consistently live up to that number-one position, and that's why I fly 60 times a year, to constantly remind the teams why we're here and relentlessly focus on the brand for the long term. I'm aware that even though there is a lot of love for the brand, there's probably a limit to how many hair ties one person can buy. So it's up to us to keep pushing on to become the go-to hair accessories brand, the most recognized in the world.

Remember the bald, middle-aged security guy at Munich airport? The one who saw 'those wiggly things' he thought looked so strange in the x-ray machine? For me, that was one of the moments I knew we were properly making it.

"Those spiral hair ties that don't leave a mark in your hair or give you headaches! Three in a cute plastic cube?" he'd said.

Here's how the rest of that conversation went with me, open-mouthed, eyebrows raised, in disbelief that a random guy would know our product.

"My wife LOVES them! She has so many. They end up under the bed in our room and every so often we have to collect a pile of them," the guy said.

*Wow.*

"Oh yes. Her favourite colour is … this one," he said, picking a three-pack of Candy Pink hair ties out of my bag.

"What do you call them again?" he said, as he zipped my bag back up. "Something like invis-ah-zu …" he tried.

"Invisibobble," I said, firmly.

"Yes. That's it. invisibobble. That simple."

And he handed my case back.

# About the Author

**Sophie Trelles-Tvede** calls herself a 'Third Culture Kid.' She was born to Spanish and Danish parents, went to school in Zurich, studied in England and now works in Munich. After founding **invisibobble** in 2012, the idea of the spiral hair tie became a true success story. In 2016, Sophie was honoured by *Forbes*' '30 under 30.'

@sophie_invisibobble

# Book Summary

When Sophie Trelles-Tvede was an 18-year-old university student, she invented the world's first spiral-shaped hair tie and called it 'invisibobble' (giving up many vodka tonics and instead investing the money she saved into her invention). Now 27, she has sold more than 100 million hair ties around the world, via 85,000 retail outlets in over 70 countries, and invisibobble turns over tens of millions of dollars a year.

*100 Million Hair Ties and a Vodka Tonic* is a behind-the-scenes look at what it's really like to build a business: what happens when your product get ruthlessly ripped off; when a ship carrying 10,000 invisibobbles burns down; when Amazon removes your entire product range just before Christmas; or when a typhoon destroys your factory in China but no one tells you about it for weeks. The secrets to invisibobble's success are largely the stories of how you recover – and now Sophie is revealing them all.